The Course of British History

Book Two

John Ray and James Hagerty

Hutchinson

London Melbourne Sydney Auckland Johannesburg

Hutchinson Education

An imprint of Century Hutchinson Ltd
62–65 Chandos Place, London WC2N 4NW

Century Hutchinson Australia Pty Ltd
PO Box 496, 16–22 Church Street, Hawthorn, Melbourne,
Victoria 3122, Australia

Century Hutchinson New Zealand Ltd
32–34 View Road, PO Box 40–086, Glenfield, Auckland 10,
New Zealand

Century Hutchinson South Africa (Pty) Ltd
PO Box 337, Bergvlei 2012, South Africa

First published 1987
© John Ray and James Hagerty 1987

Set in Palatino 11 on 13pt by Input Typesetting Ltd, London

Printed in Great Britain by
Butler & Tanner Ltd, Frome and London

British Library Cataloguing in Publication Data

Ray, John, 1929–
    British history. The course of
    Bk. 2. Tudors and Stuarts
    1. Great Britain——History
    I. Title   II. Hagerty, James
    941   DA30

ISBN 0 09 170781 1

Contents

1 England in 1485

In 1485, England had just over 3,000,000 inhabitants. Many lived in little towns, villages or hamlets scattered across the woodlands and heath that covered much of the countryside. The majority were connected with farming and the pace of their life was slower than today's. There were many fields of corn, but sheep and cattle were also kept in large numbers.

The one city of any size was London, with about 50,000 inhabitants. A foreign visitor said that it was the only place in England to compare with European cities like Rome and Florence. London had nearly a hundred churches, including the abbey at Westminster and the large St Paul's Cathedral, built in the Middle Ages. There was also the great London Bridge, carrying houses, which stretched across the Thames on nineteen arches.

Bristol, Norwich and Southampton were also important places. Most people lived in the south and east of the country, although York in the north was a thriving centre.

The visitor went on to say that Britain was divided into four sections – England, Scotland, Wales and – Cornwall! Scotland was a separate nation with its own king, James III from the

B **A family watching sheep**

House of Stuart. Wales was controlled by local lords and Ireland was governed by earls and chieftains. The kingdom was not one of the strongest states in Europe, because France and Spain were much more powerful.

A struggle for power between two groups of nobles had gone on for the previous thirty years. This hardly affected the lives of ordinary people, although many nobles were killed. But in some areas of the country, which were controlled by rich barons with their private armies, law and order had broken down.

In the countryside, farming continued as it had done since Saxon times. Villages were surrounded by three large arable fields. These fields were divided into strips so that each peasant could have a small plot of land to farm. Arable land is land on which crops can be grown, and two of the fields were used for this, while the third was left fallow (resting) for a year. Cattle were put in the meadows or on common land which could be used by all for their animals or for gathering firewood.

This was the England of 1485. Although the people of the time did not realize it, a great change was about to happen to their country. A man was coming from abroad with an army, to challenge for the English crown.

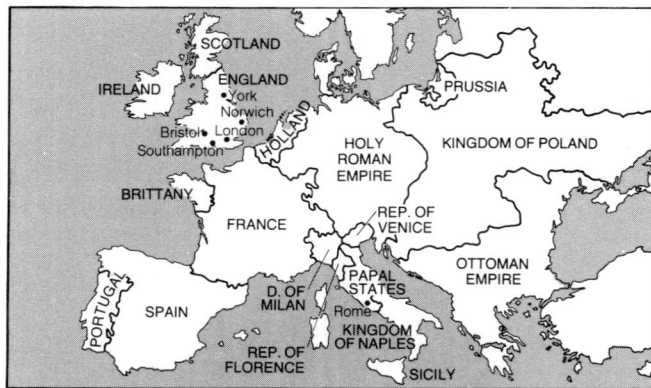

A **Britain and Western Europe in 1485**

Things to do

1 Read the chapter and answer these questions.
   (a) How many people lived in England in 1485?
   (b) How many people lived in London in 1485?
   (c) How many churches did London have in 1485?
   (d) Which cities other than London were also important?
   (e) Where did most people live?

2 (a) Copy map **A** into your book.
   (b) Underline the names of the strongest countries.

3 Using the information in the chapter and also picture **B**, explain:
   (a) the meaning of arable;
   (b) why land was divided into strips;
   (c) who could use common land;
   (d) why one field was left fallow;
   (e) what the woman in picture **B** is doing.

D The Tower of London as it was in 1483. It was a royal residence and the centre of government

4 (a) Study picture **C** and describe what you can see at *1*, *2* and *3*.
   (b) Are the people who are buying the goods rich or poor? Give reasons for your answer.

5 Look carefully at picture **D**.
   (a) Name building *1*.
   (b) Who lived in building *1*?
   (c) What appears to be happening at *2*?
   (d) Which sentence in the chapter describes *3*?
   (e) Name two buildings other than building *1* which were important.

C People shopping in a fifteenth-century market. Shoes, tableware and items of gold are on sale

6 Why do you think England was a weak nation in 1485?

2 The Battle of Bosworth, 1485

A new age in English history began in 1485 after a battle at Market Bosworth, Leicestershire. The king of England, Richard III, was killed and his army fled. The royal crown was placed on the head of his great enemy, Henry Tudor, who led the opposing army. The corpse of the king was slung over a horse and taken away.

The battle ended a struggle for power between two groups of nobles which had lasted thirty years. They were the Yorkists and the Lancastrians. Each wanted to have its own man on the throne, and the period is called the Wars of the Roses.

The Yorkists had held power with Edward IV as king from 1461 until his death in 1483. He left two sons and the elder, Prince Edward, succeeded as Edward V. Because he was so young his uncle, Richard, Duke of Gloucester, ruled as Protector of England. Soon Richard made himself king and sent his two nephews to the Tower of London. They were later put to death but there is still argument over who did this and why and how it was done.

In the meantime the chief claimant from the House of Lancaster, Henry Tudor, lived in France where he had fled fourteen years earlier. There he raised an army to invade England. He

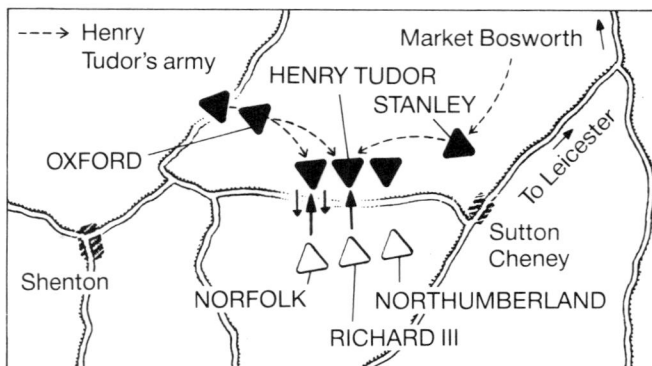

A   **Bosworth Field, 22 August 1485**

B   **Prince Edward, elder son of Edward IV**

said that if this was successful he would marry Elizabeth of York, eldest daughter of Edward IV. Thus the two houses would be united and the wars would stop.

Henry landed in Wales with an army of 3,000 Frenchmen on 1 August 1485. As he marched into England, opponents of Richard joined him. King Richard also gathered forces and called on barons with their private armies to support him. Some were not keen, fearing what would happen if they lost.

The armies met at Bosworth Field on 22 August and several noblemen waited to see which way the battle went before joining in. The fight began with a hail of arrows, then the two forces joined in battle. Richard fought bravely before being struck down. With its commander gone, his army collapsed.

Thus Henry Tudor became king of England through a surprising victory. In November he was officially crowned and two months later married Elizabeth of York. His reign was the start of the *Tudor Age* in English history.

Things to do

1 Answer **true** or **false**:
   (a) King Richard III was killed at Bosworth Field.
   (b) Richard's great friend was Henry Tudor.
   (c) Edward IV was a Yorkist king who died in 1483.
   (d) Richard became Protector and king after Edward IV.
   (e) The chief claimant for Edward's crown was Henry Tudor.

2 (a) Why did the Duke of Gloucester rule as Protector of England?
   (b) What happened to Prince Edward and Prince Richard?
   (c) What was Richard III suspected of?
   (d) Which man challenged Richard for the throne in 1485?
   (e) Why do you think this man had been living in France for fourteen years?

3 (a) What did Henry Tudor promise to do if he became king?
   (b) What would be the political result of this action?

C Richard III. He was suspected of having his nephews murdered so that he could be king

4 Imagine you are a reporter for the *Bosworth Daily Times*. Using all the information (including pictures) in the chapter, write a report on the Battle of Bosworth. Use these points: Henry Tudor landing; map of the battle; the battle; death of Richard; Henry being crowned.

5 Which promise did Henry fulfil after Bosworth?

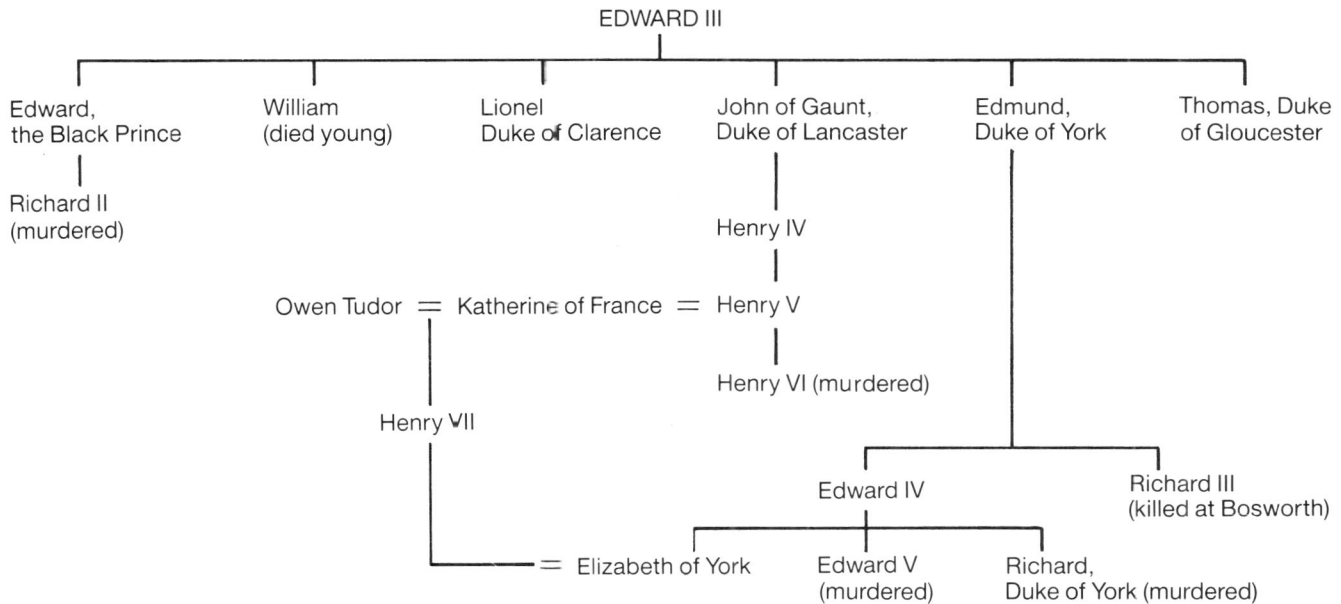

D Yorkists and Lancastrians: A family tree

3 Henry VII

Henry VII's marriage to Elizabeth of York brought the Houses of York and Lancaster together. But some Yorkists, under Margaret, the sister of Edward IV, went to live on the Continent and still opposed Henry.

Later they sent two 'pretenders' to take the English throne. These were men who claimed to be members of the royal family and wanted to overthrow Henry, but he dealt with them easily. The first, Lambert Simnel, was sent to work in the royal kitchens. Perkin Warbeck, the other, was captured and later killed.

One of Henry's greatest problems was how to bring law and order to England. He had to limit the power of his 'overmighty subjects', the barons. This he did through his own courts, where they had to pay large fines for small offences. They were not allowed to keep their private armies and few were chosen as the king's advisers. The barons soon realized that King Henry was determined to control them and they had to obey the law.

The new king strengthened his position with other lands. He did this by arranging marriages between his children and those of the rulers of other European nations. His daughter, Margaret, married the King of Scotland. His eldest son, Arthur, married Catherine of Aragon, a Spanish princess.

Henry encouraged peace through trade as well. There was a large demand for English woollen

B A portrait of King Henry VII holding the red rose of Lancaster, painted shortly before his death

cloth and he obtained good trading treaties for merchants. He helped shipping by insisting that some goods were to be carried only in English vessels.

The king also aided the Cabots, Italian explorers searching for a way to the East across the Atlantic Ocean. This started English interest in the north-east coast of America.

Henry was an active man, enjoying hunting and life at Court. His wife Elizabeth died in 1503 after giving birth to a child, and the king lived on to 1509.

At his death, England was far stronger than in 1485. Henry was shrewd and careful in building a strong nation. He had also made a personal fortune which was passed on to his successor. Prince Arthur had died, so the heir to the throne was the younger son who became Henry VIII.

A A medal to mark the occasion of the wedding of Henry Tudor to Elizabeth of York on 18 January 1486

Things to do

1 Copy and complete these sentences using the words from the Word List.
   (a) Henry VII married —— of ——.
   (b) The House of York was united to the House of ——.
   (c) The 'Pretenders' claimed to be members of the —— ——.
   (d) —— —— was captured and later ——.
   (e) Henry brought —— and —— to England.

   Word List
   law York Lancaster royal order
   Elizabeth Perkin family Warbeck killed

2 (a) Who can you see in picture **D**?
   (b) What did he pretend to be?
   (c) What happened to him?

3 Explain how Henry VII:
   (a) controlled the barons;
   (b) strengthened his position with other lands;
   (c) encouraged peace through trade.

4 What is your opinion of Henry VII as a king? Give reasons for your answer.

D Perkin Warbeck, who claimed to be a member of the royal family and claimed Henry's crown

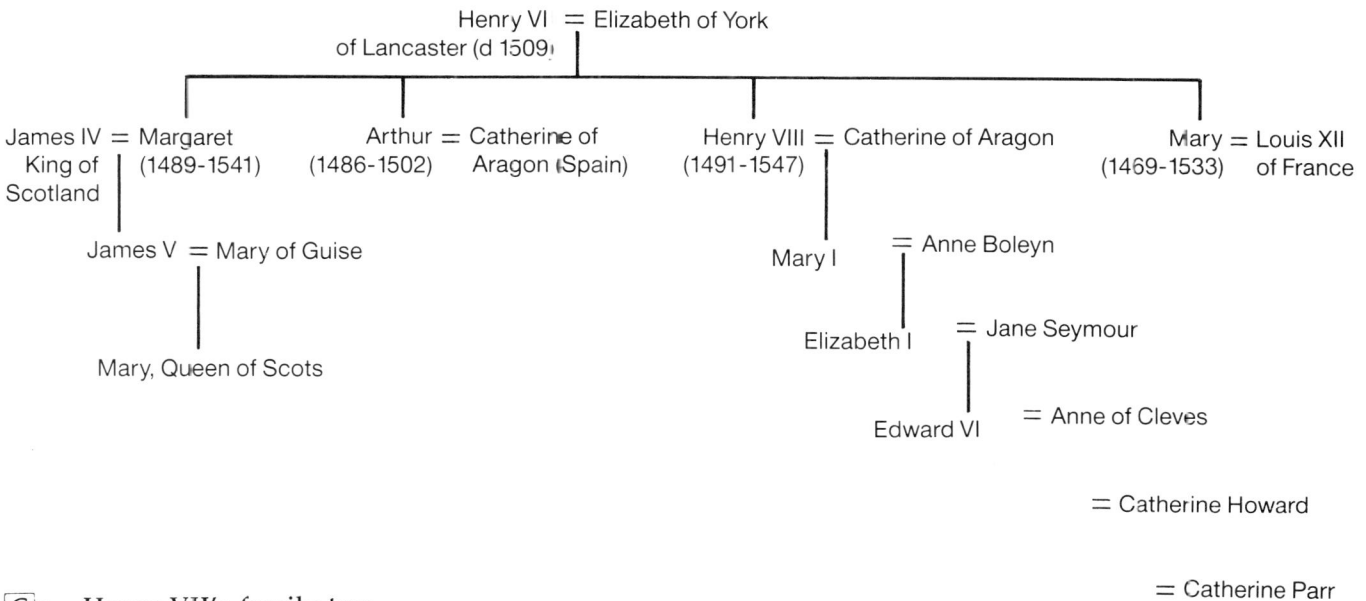

Henry VI = Elizabeth of York
of Lancaster (d 1509)

James IV = Margaret (1489-1541)
King of Scotland

Arthur = Catherine of Aragon (Spain)
(1486-1502)

Henry VIII = Catherine of Aragon
(1491-1547)

Mary = Louis XII
(1469-1533) of France

James V = Mary of Guise

Mary I

= Anne Boleyn

Elizabeth I

= Jane Seymour

Mary, Queen of Scots

Edward VI

= Anne of Cleves

= Catherine Howard

= Catherine Parr

C Henry VII's family tree

4 The Renaissance

There are some periods in history which are remembered because so much happens in a short time. One of those ages came between 1400 and 1550, when important changes occurred to alter many people's thoughts and outlook on life. It was an age of discovery and exploration. New ideas about religion were discussed. Some of the world's greatest art, sculpture and architecture were produced.

The period is often called 'The Renaissance'. The word renaissance means 'rebirth', or 'being born again'. This stage of history marks the end of the Middle Ages and the beginning of Modern Times.

First of all, what happened in the Renaissance? People began to study again the thoughts, works and writings of the Ancient Greeks and Romans. They saw that much could be learned about such things as sculpture, architecture, medicine, poetry and religion by examining the works of the past. Scholars began to question what they had been taught. They enquired deeply into science and astronomy, geography and art.

Much of this study began in Italy, in rich cities like Florence and Rome where people could often see works of the past. In 1453 the Turks captured the city of Constantinople. Many of the scholars who lived there had a great knowledge of the Ancient Greeks and the Romans. Some of them then went to Italy and helped to spread the teaching about the past which had already begun there. From Italy travellers carried the new ideas to other European countries.

About 1450 an invention was made in Europe which helped the new ideas to spread more quickly. This was the printing press. Johann Gutenberg in Germany made movable type. In 1476 William Caxton introduced printing to

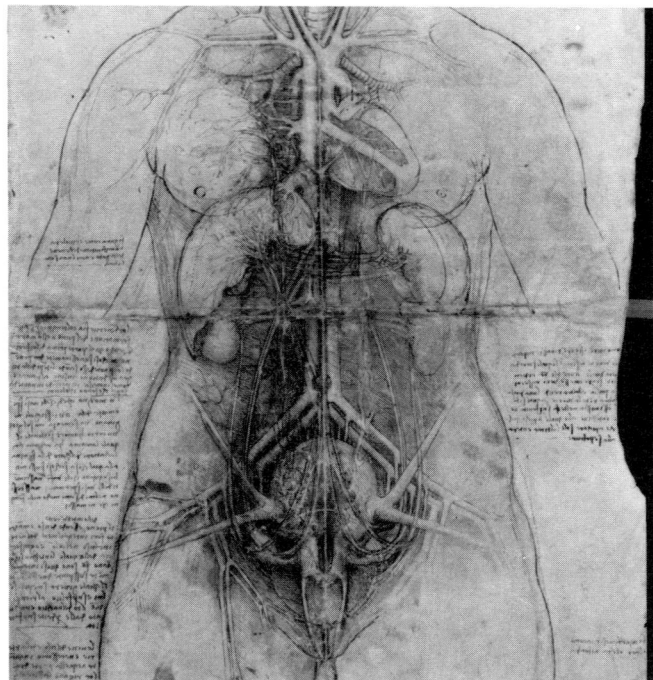

A Leonardo da Vinci (1452–1519) was one of the first artists to study the workings of the human body so that he could make his drawings as realistic as possible

England, setting up his press near Westminster Abbey. This invention meant that books could be produced in larger numbers and gradually more people could learn to read them.

The thoughts and writings, buildings and art of the Renaissance are among the most wonderful achievements ever made. For example, in painting there were the Italians, Botticelli and Michelangelo, who was also a sculptor and architect. Leonardo da Vinci was a poet, musician, architect and scientist. Copernicus, a Pole, and Galileo, an Italian, helped to start the science of astronomy.

All of these men and many others brought in a new age of learning. Gradually it affected all countries in western Europe, including Britain.

Things to do

1 Quick questions:
   (a) What does Renaissance mean?
   (b) When did the Renaissance take place?
   (c) Where did the Renaissance begin?
   (d) Which ancient peoples did scholars learn about?
   (e) How were new ideas carried to other countries?

2 (a) Study picture **C** carefully and draw five different shapes which you can see in the building (for example, a circle).
   (b) Can you name other buildings with these shapes?

3 Study picture **B**.
   (a) Who do you think the man at *1* is?
   (b) What can you see at *2*?
   (c) What are the men at *3* and *4* doing?
   (d) List the other jobs being done.
   (e) Why was printing so important?

4 Study picture **D** and write down the time it takes for the earth (la Terre) and Saturn to go round the sun.

5 Make a list of five inventions or changes (for example, television) and say how each one has affected people's lives.

C The Church of San Andrea, Italy, a mixture of Greek and Roman styles. Notice the different shapes within the building

B A printing shop. Early printing was a very slow process, but it enabled the spread of ideas through books

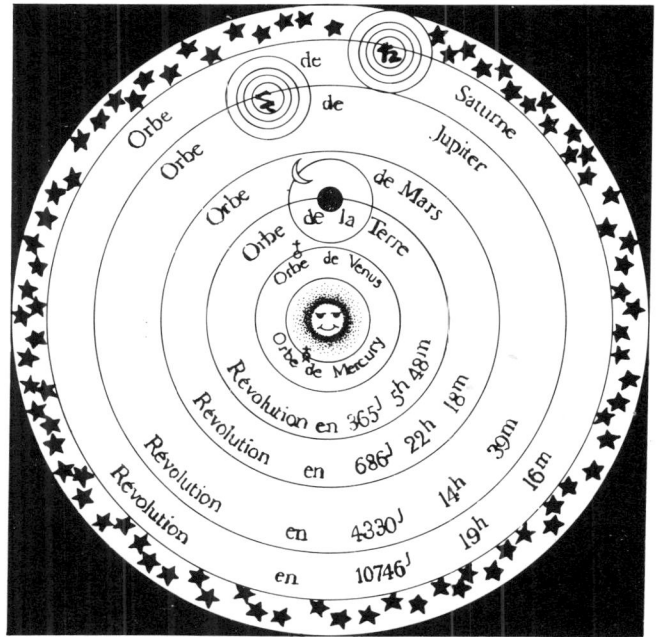

D Copernicus showed that the planets of the solar system, including the earth, moved around the sun

5 The Reformation

The Renaissance caused people to think more freely and to question things they had been taught. New ideas began to spread about religion. The Roman Catholic Church had been the only Church in western Europe for more than a thousand years. But the new thoughts led to changes, many of which occurred between 1500 and 1550. In several countries people spoke out against the Roman Catholic Church and its teaching. Some broke away and formed their own Churches in their own lands. They would no longer obey the Pope in Rome.

This movement is called 'The Reformation'. Those who wanted to change the Roman Catholic Church said they were trying to *reform* it. They *protested* against some of its teaching and the bad example set by some of its leaders. Therefore these people were known as *Protestants*.

Protestants thought that much evil existed in the Roman Catholic Church, pointing out that some of its teachings were wrong. They believed that some of its leaders cared more for worldly goods than for preaching about Christianity. In their view there should be new ways of worshipping God.

In 1517 a German monk named Martin Luther led a revolt against the Roman Catholic Church, to which he belonged. He announced that people should have faith in God's love and mercy towards them, which He had shown by sending His Son, Jesus Christ, to live in the world. Luther said that all the ceremonies, buildings and wealth of the Church did not matter as much as faith.

Naturally these statements angered the Pope, who ordered Luther to go to Rome for questioning. The German refused, so the Pope expelled him from the Roman Catholic Church.

A The Church in England before the Reformation. You may like to count the important churches, abbeys and monasteries. Do you live near one?

Over the following fifty years the Reformation affected many countries in Europe. Groups of people there followed Luther's example, speaking and writing against the Roman Catholic Church and breaking away from it. They founded their own Churches. This happened in Germany, Holland and Sweden, and it also occurred in England and Scotland.

However, other countries such as Spain, Ireland and Italy did not change their loyalty to the Roman Catholic Church. They remained as strongholds of support for the Pope.

The changes led to great bitterness between Protestants and Catholics. In some places there were wars of religion lasting into the seventeenth century.

Things to do

B Martin Luther, the German monk who led the revolt against the Roman Catholic Church

1 Read the chapter then copy and complete these sentences:
   (a) The Roman Catholic Church had been ———.
   (b) In several countries people ———.
   (c) Some broke away and ———.
   (d) They would no longer ———.
   (e) This movement is called ———.

2 List three complaints which the Protestants had against the Roman Catholic Church.

3 (a) What did Martin Luther preach?
   (b) What was the Pope's reply?
   (c) List the countries where people broke away from the Roman Catholic Church.
   (d) Which European countries stayed loyal to the Roman Catholic Church?
   (e) What did these differences lead to?

4 Look at the three maps in picture **C**. Explain the differences between each map.

C

(a) Catholic Europe in 1500

(b) Europe during the Reformation

(c) Europe in 1600

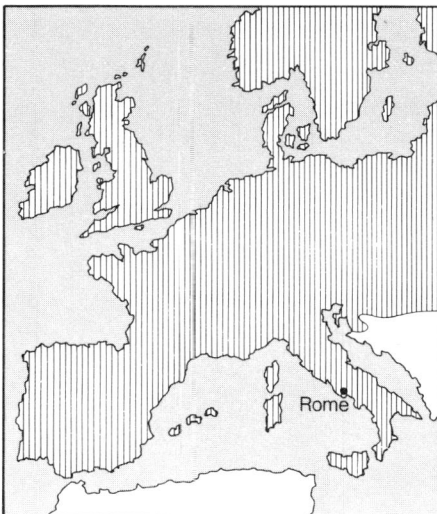

Roman Catholic

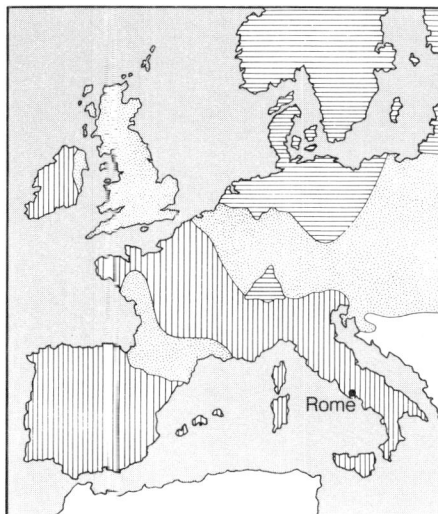

Chiefly Roman Catholic   Mixed
Chiefly Protestant

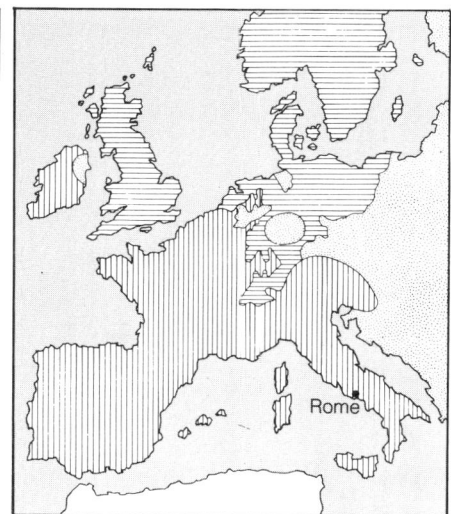

Chiefly Roman Catholic   Mixed
Chiefly Protestant

6 Henry VIII, to 1530

King Henry VIII reigned from 1509 until 1547

Henry VIII became king in 1509, aged eighteen. His father had left him a strong kingdom, with sound finance and no more dangers from the Wars of the Roses. He married Catherine of Aragon to whom he had been engaged for several years. At first the young king enjoyed his new power and position, with hunting, feasting, dancing and jousting. So he left much of the government of England to others.

One very able servant was Thomas Wolsey. Although he came from a humble background, he had made rapid progress. He entered the Roman Catholic Church and soon showed his abilities, so was given great power by Henry.

In particular Wolsey had dealings with foreign countries like Spain and France. He hoped to improve England's position in Europe and, at the same time, achieve his own ambition. He wanted to become Pope, leader of all Roman Catholics.

Wolsey also grew powerful in England. He heard law cases and imposed fines, and soon was second only to Henry. Wolsey lived in great state and grew unpopular with some people at Court. He became Lord Chancellor, then was made a Cardinal (a high position in the Roman Catholic Church). In 1518, he was appointed to be the Pope's personal representative in England.

His downfall occurred more than ten years later, over 'The King's Matter'. Catherine of Aragon had produced seven children but only one – a daughter named Mary – had lived. Henry wanted a son to succeed him. Not only that, he had also fallen in love with Anne Boleyn, a lady of the Court.

In 1527 Wolsey was told to obtain a divorce for the king from the only person who could grant it – Pope Clement VII. However, the Pope did not want to offend either Henry or Catherine, so he kept putting off his decision.

Matters moved so slowly that in May 1529 Henry lost his temper and blamed Wolsey for the failure. The king's loyal servant was dismissed and his wealth taken. Wolsey retired to York, but in 1530 he was charged with treason and ordered to London for trial. He got as far south as Leicester Abbey but was too ill to proceed. Wolsey died there in complete disgrace.

The king was now faced with a great problem as worries grew in his personal life. He had dismissed Wolsey, but he still needed to obtain a divorce. How was he to get it?

Anne Boleyn, whom Henry wished to marry

Things to do

1 Name the people you can see in pictures **A**, **B** and **C**.

2 (a) Which person became King of England in 1509?
  (b) Which man became Lord Chancellor and a Cardinal?
  (c) Which person did the king wish to divorce?
  (d) With whom had the king fallen in love?
  (e) Which person could grant a divorce to the king?

D Cardinal Thomas Wolsey. He rose from a poor background to become the King's chief minister and a Cardinal of the Roman Catholic Church

C Catherine of Aragon was Henry's first wife. She had been married to his brother Arthur, who died

3 (a) Why did Henry wish to divorce Catherine?
  (b) Why did the Pope avoid making a decision?
  (c) Why was Wolsey dismissed?

4 Imagine you are Henry VIII. Write a short description of your life at the start of your reign. Here are some clues: strong kingdom, hunting and feasting, falling in love, divorce.

5 Write a brief account of Cardinal Wolsey's life.

7 Henry VIII, 1530 – 47

By 1530 the Reformation was spreading in England, and the Roman Catholic Church was becoming unpopular with some people. It was a rich and powerful Church. Often its churchmen failed to do the duties they were paid for. The Pope was an Italian, and many English people disliked foreigners.

So when Henry VIII argued with the Pope over his marriage, most people supported him. He decided to make himself Head of the Catholic Church in England (which became known as the Church of England), then go ahead with his divorce.

Henry used Parliament to do this. Between 1529 and 1536 they passed laws to remove the power of the Pope. However, no changes were made in what people were allowed to believe about religion.

Anyone who opposed Henry was punished. Even Sir Thomas More, a former friend, was beheaded for refusing to recognize the king as Head of the Church.

When Henry had divorced Catherine of Aragon, he married Anne Boleyn. He tired of her after she had a daughter, Elizabeth, and accused her of having affairs with other men. Anne was beheaded, then he married Jane Seymour. She produced Edward, the son Henry longed for, but she died soon afterwards.

The king used Thomas Cromwell, a ruthless but loyal man, to attack the Pope's power in England. As royal secretary, Cromwell took steps to increase Henry's strength and wealth.

Monks and nuns were the Pope's main supporters. Knowing this, between 1536 and 1540 Cromwell closed, or 'dissolved', the monasteries. The occupants were given a

A Byland Abbey, Yorkshire, one of the many monasteries 'dissolved' by Henry. Its land, money and buildings provided Henry with much wealth

pension, then their lands, buildings, money and treasures were taken for the king, who sold them off. Anyone who resisted was punished; some were hanged.

There were other changes. Thomas Cranmer, the Archbishop of Canterbury, and Cromwell arranged that Bibles written in English, not Latin, were placed in all churches.

But Henry was still a Catholic. Although Catholics were put to death if they opposed his supreme position, Protestants could also be killed for disagreeing with the teachings of the Catholic Church.

Henry had three more wives. After Jane Seymour's death, he married Anne of Cleves, but the marriage broke up. Then he married Catherine Howard, who was beheaded for unfaithfulness. Finally, his last wife was Catherine Parr, who was still alive at his death.

When Thomas Cromwell had outlived his usefulness, he was beheaded. Henry VIII grew old, ill and immensely fat, but he never lost his commanding position in England, where he was both loved and feared. In 1547 he died, after a reign which was a turning point in English history.

Things to do

1 Read the chapter and then name:
   (a) the king's former friend who was beheaded;
   (b) the royal secretary who attacked the Pope's power;
   (c) the Archbishop who introduced new Bibles;
   (d) the king's six wives;
   (e) the king who died in 1547.

2 List three reasons why English people might have supported Henry in his quarrel with the Pope and the Roman Catholic Church.

3 (a) Study picture **B** and name persons *1* and *2*.
   (b) What are they standing on?
   (c) Describe, in your own words, the meaning of the cartoon.

4 In picture **D** you can see Thomas More and his family. Which office did More hold and why was he beheaded?

5 What happened to places like Byland Abbey?

C Archbishop Thomas Cranmer was prepared to support Henry. He became the first Anglican (Church of England) Archbishop of Canterbury

6 (a) Who was Thomas Cromwell?
   (b) How did Cranmer support the king?
   (c) Did Henry remain Catholic? Give reasons to support your answer.
   (d) Henry VIII had six wives. What problems do you think this could lead to after his death?

B Henry VIII and Cranmer trampling the Pope's decrees underfoot

D Thomas More, Henry's Lord Chancellor and chief minister, surrounded by his family. More refused to support Henry in his quarrel with the Pope

8 The 'Mary Rose'

On 19 July 1545, the warship *Mary Rose* sailed into action against a French fleet off Portsmouth. Suddenly she heeled over, water poured in through the open gun-ports, and the 700-ton vessel went down in minutes. Aboard there were 700 sailors and soldiers, ready for action, yet only forty were saved.

Over the centuries a few timbers and guns were recovered, but the ship lay silted up on the seabed less than a mile offshore. Fortunately the silt preserved the wreck.

The *Mary Rose* was re-discovered in 1971 by underwater archaeologists and was raised in 1982. Remains of the vessel and its contents are now displayed in a Portsmouth museum. They form the most valuable sunken treasure ever found in British waters.

Historians have learned much because the ship sank so quickly into silt, on the point of fighting a battle. For example, the hull and rigging show that she was one of the world's first sailing warships. The *Mary Rose* carried ninety-one bronze or wrought-iron guns. All were ready to fire, some with iron shot, others with stone or lead shot. From the guns recovered, sailors have discovered more about fighting methods at sea.

In 1545 archers were still important in battle, and there were many on the vessel. Over 130 bows and 2,000 arrows were found, so obviously English bowmen were to have played a large part in the fight.

Hundreds of small items have revealed details of everyday life in Tudor times. The sailors had their personal belongings with them: their sleeveless leather jerkins, woollen tights and shoes or boots.

They played with dice and gaming-boards, or draughts in their spare time. Several musical pipes and a drum were found. One sailor had a whippet dog which died with his master.

Food was recovered. They ate fish, beef, venison and mutton, fresh peas and plums. Officers drank wine while the men had ale.

The surgeon's cabin contained ointments and syringes, a saw and wooden jars. He would have been very busy in battle.

Hundreds of other items are now on display. The sinking of the *Mary Rose* was a disaster at the time, but underwater archaeologists have given us the chance to learn from it.

A   Tudor warships in action off Portsmouth

Things to do

1 Match up the phrases in column A with those in column B.

A	B
(a) When the *Mary Rose* sank	ninety-one bronze or wrought-iron guns and was raised in 1982
(b) The *Mary Rose* was fighting	there were 700 men on board
(c) The *Mary Rose* carried	are now displayed in a Portsmouth museum
(d) The *Mary Rose* was found in 1971	against a French fleet
(e) Remains of the *Mary Rose*	

2 Copy map **B** to show where the *Mary Rose* sank.

3 Imagine you had been at Southsea Castle on 19 July 1545. Using the chapter describe the scene and the sinking of the *Mary Rose*.

4 What do you think would have been (a) the advantages and (b) the disadvantages of wooden, sail-powered warships?

B

Where the *Mary Rose* sank

C The wreck of the *Mary Rose* being lifted out of the sea on 11 October 1982

5 Imagine you were an underwater archaeologist.
  (a) What would have been your thoughts as the wreck was raised?
  (b) List the items recovered from the *Mary Rose* and say what you consider to be the five most interesting ones. Give reasons for your answer.

D An artist's impression of the inside of a Tudor warship

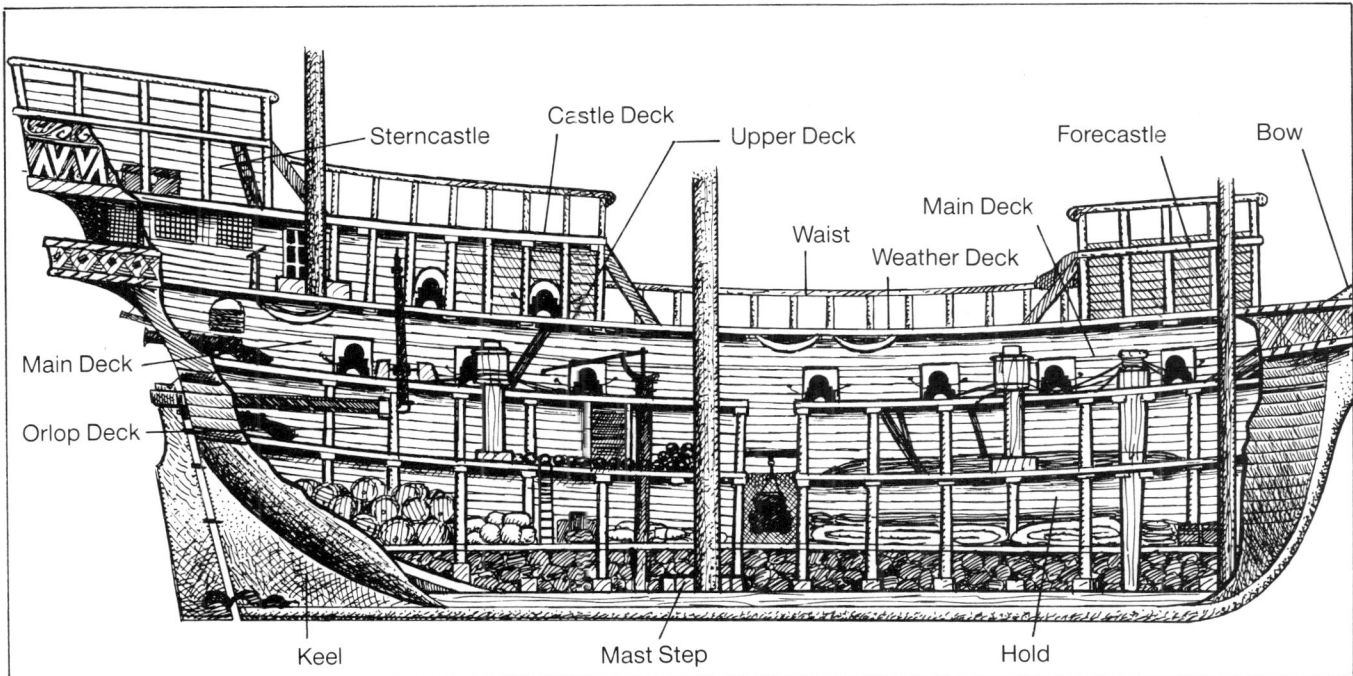

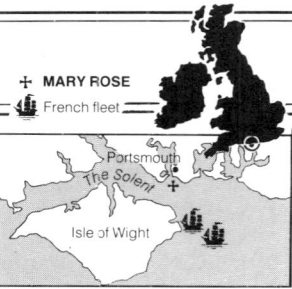

Sterncastle — Castle Deck — Upper Deck — Forecastle — Bow — Main Deck — Waist — Weather Deck — Main Deck — Orlop Deck — Keel — Mast Step — Hold

9 Edward VI

When Henry VIII died he left three children. The two older ones were girls: Mary and Elizabeth. The third, Edward, was only nine years old, but being a boy, he succeeded to the throne. Henry had arranged that when he died, a Council would govern for his son.

The leader of that Council was Edward Seymour, Duke of Somerset, the new king's uncle. He was given the title of 'Protector'.

His nephew Edward, who was a frail boy in health, loved learning and study. Although young, he was keenly interested in religion. Now the Protestants started to make further changes in the Church.

The first Prayer Book in English was introduced in 1549, and clergymen were forced to use it. In some churches pictures were painted over and statues removed because they were considered to be idols.

Many Catholics were offended, and in 1549 there were uprisings in the West Country and Wales. The rebels there wanted the old religion and would not accept change. The government sent soldiers who crushed the opposition.

The Duke of Somerset had to deal with a great evil of the age: the poverty suffered by many country people. It had more than one cause. To start with, there wasn't so much work to be had. Landowners all over England had been turning their estates to pasture for sheep instead of growing crops, because there was money to be made from keeping sheep and selling their wool. The sheep were easier to look after than crops, so fewer labourers were needed.

In some places, common land meant for ordinary people to grow crops on was enclosed

A King Edward VI (1547–53) was nine years of age when he succeeded his father

by the landowners for keeping sheep. So the poorer people suffered, because they depended on the food crops grown on common land.

In East Anglia an uprising against the enclosure of land led to bloodshed, and 300 rebels were executed. It also led to the downfall of the Duke of Somerset, who was accused by landowners of encouraging the rebellion by criticizing enclosure.

The Protector who took his place was the Duke of Northumberland. Under his rule the Church became more Protestant. Ornaments and vestments (robes worn for special ceremonies) were taken, statues and paintings destroyed. A second Prayer Book was introduced, encouraged by the young king who was a keen reformer.

Edward suffered from tuberculosis (a disease which affects the lungs), and died in 1553. By Henry VIII's will, his sister Mary was to succeed – but she was a Catholic. Protestants saw her as a threat.

Because of this, Northumberland persuaded Edward to make a will. He then forged it to leave the crown to his own daughter-in-law, Lady Jane Grey.

But at Edward's death more and more people supported Mary's claim. As she approached London, Northumberland surrendered to her and was put in the Tower.

Things to do

1. Study picture **B** and answer these questions by referring to the chapter:
   - (a) Who is person *1*?
   - (b) How old was person *1* when he became king?
   - (c) Who is person *2*?
   - (d) What title did person *2* have?
   - (e) Why did he have this title?

2. (a) What changes did Protestants make in the churches?
   - (b) Who was upset by these changes?
   - (c) What happened in 1549?

3. (a) What 'great evil of the age' did the Duke of Somerset have to deal with?
   - (b) What effect did the enclosure of land have on poor people?
   - (c) What happened in East Anglia?
   - (d) Why did Northumberland replace Somerset?

4. (a) In what ways did the English Church became more Protestant because of Northumberland?
   - (b) How was Mary a threat to English Protestants?
   - (c) Why was Northumberland put into the Tower of London?

B Edward (1) and his Council of Ministers. Somerset (2) was made 'Protector' and was leader of the Council

C The interior of a Protestant church during Edward's reign

D The interior of a Roman Catholic Church during the same period

10 Mary I

Mary became queen in 1553, at the age of thirty-seven. She never forgot her sufferings as a child when her father, Henry VIII, divorced her mother, Catherine of Aragon. She had seen the power of the Roman Catholic Church rapidly decline in England as Protestants took over, and she was determined to change religion back to what it had been.

At first she was popular, because people did not trust the Duke of Northumberland. Soon he was executed, and Mary then took steps to restore the Roman Catholic Church in England. Two Catholic bishops, Gardiner and Bonner, were released from prison and became her advisers. Several Protestant bishops were sent to the Tower. Services in Latin were brought back in churches.

Mary believed that if she married a Catholic, it would strengthen her position and would also help the Church. She chose Philip of Spain, hoping that the marriage would unite England with her mother's homeland. However, some English people did not want a foreigner on the throne, so in January 1554 there was a rebellion, led by Sir Thomas Wyatt. He intended to overthrow Mary and offer the crown to Elizabeth, but the uprising failed.

As a result of the rebellion, there were many executions, including Lady Jane Grey and her husband, who were still a threat to Mary's position. Princess Elizabeth was imprisoned in the Tower, although she took no part in the plot.

Philip, eleven years younger than Mary, came to England. They were married in Winchester Cathedral, and then she set about restoring her nation to the Roman Catholic faith.

Parliament did away with Acts that had given such power to Henry VIII. Then they attacked

A Queen Mary, daughter of Henry VIII and Catherine of Aragon

Protestant opponents, accusing them of heresy (disagreeing with the teachings of the Catholic Church). Heretics were burned at the stake, whether they were clergymen or ordinary citizens. Fear of burning led some people to hide their true beliefs, but others were prepared to die bravely.

Between 1555 and 1558 about 300 Protestants were burned. Some were Church leaders, like Thomas Cranmer, Archbishop of Canterbury, but many were ordinary men and women who died courageously. Those watching the executions felt bitter towards the authorities, and the persecutions strengthened Protestant feelings.

Mary grew more unhappy. She had no children, and her husband Philip went back to Spain. The French occupied Calais, England's last possession in France. The queen grew ill and died in November 1558.

Things to do

1 Read the chapter then copy and complete these sentences:
   (a) Mary's father was —— and her mother was —— .
   (b) Mary took steps to restore the —— in England.
   (c) Philip of —— became —— husband.
   (d) Mary had —— imprisoned and —— executed.
   (e) Between 1555 and 1558 many —— were burned for their faith.

2 (a) If you were a Catholic why would you support Mary's marriage to Philip of Spain?
   (b) If you were a Protestant why would you oppose Mary's marriage to Philip of Spain?

3 Study picture **B** and explain;
   (a) who the prisoners are;
   (b) why they have been arrested;
   (c) what might have happened to them.

B Protestants in Colchester being arrested as heretics (those who did not agree with Catholicism). Some were tortured and others were executed

4 Imagine that you witnessed the execution of Thomas Cranmer, Archbishop of Canterbury. Write an entry into your diary describing the scene and recording your feelings.

5 What effect do you think such executions had upon ordinary people and how would Catholics and Protestants feel about each other?

C Lady Jane Grey was a threat to Mary, and was executed

D Philip II of Spain, Mary's Catholic husband

11 Elizabeth I

Elizabeth was twenty-five years old when she succeeded her half-sister Mary in 1558. Her reign became one of the longest and most eventful in England's story.

She was born and brought up during stormy years of change. Her mother, Anne Boleyn, had been beheaded and she herself was harshly treated. She had seen many people, Catholic and Protestant, executed for their views. During Mary's reign she had been kept in the Tower for two months.

This background made Elizabeth into a careful, shrewd woman. England had passed through a troubled age and she needed to guide her country carefully. Particularly she wanted the love and respect of her people.

Elizabeth had received a good education. She understood Greek and Latin and spoke several languages. Singing, playing music and dancing all gave her pleasure.

She was tall, with reddish-gold hair, and was attractive rather than beautiful. She became popular with her subjects, who served her loyally. She could be dignified and firm in an age when women had little power.

In 1558 her first great problem was religion, which had caused so much bloodshed in previous years. She avoided trouble by being moderate. Acts were passed which satisfied Protestants and Catholics for many years. She took the title 'Supreme Governor' instead of 'Supreme Head' of the Church. People not attending church were fined.

Much help was given to the queen by William Cecil. He was her wise adviser right through her reign, till his death in 1598.

A Elizabeth I in Parliament. Facing her are the MPs (foot of picture), the bishops of the Church of England (left), and the lords (right)

Many English people wanted Elizabeth to marry so there could be an heir to the throne and less danger from abroad. A number of foreign princes were very interested and proposals came from France and Spain, Sweden and Austria. But Elizabeth never married. She felt a strong duty towards governing England and believed she would lose power through marriage.

Possibly she loved Robert Dudley who was already married. After his wife's strange death, Elizabeth would not marry him because scandal could have weakened her position.

She was very popular with the ordinary people in England. Elizabeth liked to visit different parts of the country so that they could see her, and citizens turned out to cheer the royal procession as it went by.

Things to do

1 Look at picture **A**.
   (a) What kind of men would be there in front of the queen?
   (b) Name the man in picture **D** who advised Elizabeth.
   (c) What was the queen's first great problem?
   (d) How did Elizabeth avoid trouble between Catholics and Protestants?
   (e) What would happen to you if you did not go to church?

2 (a) Who was Elizabeth's father?
   (b) Who was Elizabeth's mother?

3 Look at picture **B** and underneath it write down a list of words or phrases used in the chapter to describe her (for example 'careful, shrewd').

4 Explain:
   (a) why English people wanted Elizabeth to marry; and
   (b) why she never did marry.

5 How do you think Elizabeth's upbringing and early life affected her as queen?

B Queen Elizabeth I dressed in splendour, wearing a crown and holding the orb and sceptre which were the symbols of monarchy

C Religion was a problem for Elizabeth. Roman Catholic priests such as Robert Parsons and Edmund Campion (shown here) were smuggled into England. To be captured meant death. Campion was hanged

D William Cecil, Lord Burghley, who advised Elizabeth for forty years

12 Mary, Queen of Scots

Mary Stuart, Queen of Scots, was a remarkable woman. Her grandmother was Margaret, eldest daughter of Henry VII, who had married James IV of Scotland. Therefore Mary had a claim to the English throne.

She became queen of Scotland at her father's death when she was six days old. At the age of six, Mary was sent to France, Scotland's traditional ally, to be brought up as a French Roman Catholic princess, and there she married the king's son. By the time she was seventeen she was queen of both Scotland and France.

Mary was then an important person in Europe, claiming also the crown of England because Elizabeth was illegitimate in the eyes of Roman Catholics. This argument went on for years, ending only with her death.

Her young husband died tragically in 1560 and she returned to Scotland. She was very popular, although by then many Scots had become Protestant, while she was a devout Roman Catholic. The Protestant leader, John Knox, disliked her but she did not interfere in religion.

Troubles started when she married a cousin, the Earl of Darnley. He was selfish and ambitious and one night had her Italian secretary, David Rizzio, killed near her at Holyrood Palace because he was jealous of their relationship.

Later, while Mary was away, Darnley's house was blown up. His body was found nearby – strangled. The mystery has never been solved but blame fell on Mary's latest admirer, the Earl of Bothwell. Soon Mary married him after he had divorced his wife.

Protestant lords rebelled and Mary was driven out of Scotland, whose crown was given to her

A Mary, Queen of Scots, daughter of James V of Scotland and Mary of Guise. She was descended from Henry VII

young son, as James VI. The queen herself fled to England and begged for help from Elizabeth.

Elizabeth's position was difficult. She would not allow another queen to be harmed – but Mary was a rival for her throne. So Mary was given refuge, but was not allowed to travel about freely.

Soon, Catholics in England plotted to overthrow Elizabeth and make Mary queen. These plots went on for years, especially after 1570 when the Pope announced that Catholics should no longer regard Elizabeth as their rightful queen.

In 1586, evidence was produced that Mary was deeply involved in yet another plot. A death warrant was signed and she was beheaded at Fotheringhay Castle in February 1587.

Just before execution, however, Mary passed on her claim to the English throne to Philip of Spain. Before long, Elizabeth was faced by a new threat to her position.

Things to do

1 (a) Name the people in pictures **A** and **B**.
   (b) Name the country where Mary was brought up.
   (c) Name Mary's second husband.
   (d) Name the man suspected of killing Darnley.
   (e) Name the person who succeeded Mary as ruler of Scotland.

2 Using the information in this chapter, and referring back to chapter 3, explain how Mary was descended from Henry VII.

3 Why did Mary claim the English throne?

4 Imagine you are Elizabeth I. Complete two lists – 'For' and 'Against'. Under 'For' write down the reasons why you should help Mary. Under 'Against' write down the reasons why you should not help her.

5 Study picture **D**. Write a report to Queen Elizabeth describing the event.

B Henry Stuart, Lord Darnley (right), with his younger brother Charles

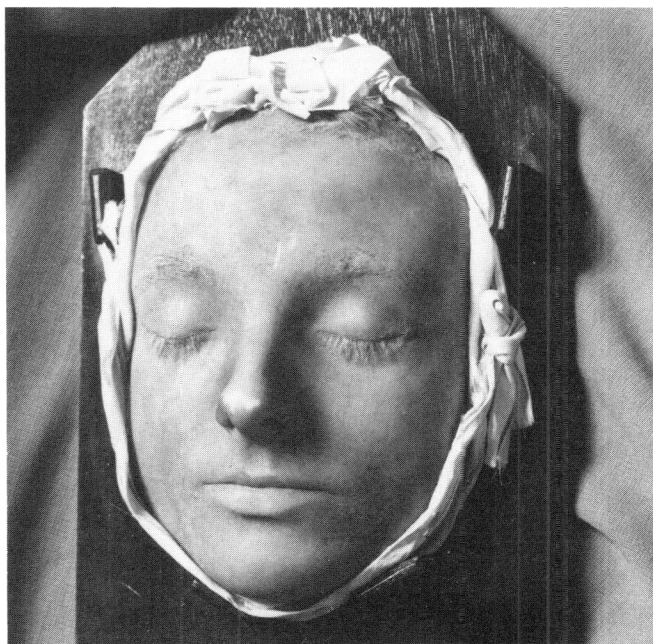

C The death mask of Mary. She was aged forty-five

D The execution of Mary at Fotheringhay Castle. She met her death with courage and dignity

27

13 Explorers and trade routes

By 1450 trade between Europe and the Far East had existed for centuries. Caravans of camels and horses made their way across Central Asia, following 'The Silk Road'. They brought silks and fine cloths, spices and precious stones from Cathay (China), India and Cipangu (Japan) to sell to Europeans.

This trade was blocked in the mid-fifteenth century by the Turks, who attacked south-eastern Europe. In 1453 they captured the city of Constantinople, an important trading centre, so Europeans started searching for a sea route to the Far East.

The first route, explored by the Portuguese, went round the southern cape of Africa, then across the Indian Ocean. In 1498 Vasco da Gama reached India. His voyage opened a rich trade with the Far East for Portuguese merchants.

A Genoese sailor, Christopher Columbus, also wanted to reach the East. He was one of the first to believe that the world is round. So he planned to sail westwards and reach China that way. The Spanish king gave him help, and he sailed in 1492. Columbus arrived in the West Indies which *he* thought were near India.

Spanish explorers soon realized that an unknown continent was nearby. They found gold and silver, and carefully guarded this rich trade with 'The New World' – America.

In 1493 the Pope divided these newly discovered lands between Spain and Portugal by drawing a line on a map. The Portuguese were awarded all territories to the east and the Spanish all to the west. Naturally, sailors of other lands were angry at this ruling.

English interest began in 1497 when John Cabot of Genoa sailed west from Bristol for Henry VII,

A Christopher Columbus meets natives of the West Indies. He wrote this account in his diary: 'That we might form a great friendship, for I knew that they were a people who could be more easily converted to our Holy Faith by love than by force. I gave to some of them red caps and glass beads to put around their necks, and many other things of little value, which gave them great pleasure, and made them as much our friends that it was a marvel to see.'

hoping to find China. He failed, but reached Newfoundland and Labrador where there were fishing grounds.

The Portuguese explorer, Ferdinand Magellan, was the first to sail right round the world. His voyage lasted three years.

In 1553 Hugh Willoughby and Richard Chancellor tried to reach the East by sailing north-eastward round Russia. They were unsuccessful, but Chancellor founded the Muscovy Company and traded with the Russians.

Further south, English sailors clashed with Spaniards on trade routes. This led to the most remarkable voyage of the Tudor Age when Francis Drake led the first English expedition to sail round the world.

Things to do

1 Copy map **C** into your book.

2 As an English sailor, why would you object to the Pope's dividing new lands between Spain and Portugal?

B A sixteenth-century map of Africa

3 Copy and complete this chart:

The Explorers

Name	Country discovered
Vasco da Gama	India
Columbus	
Cabot	
Magellan	
Chancellor	

4 Why did Europeans search for a new sea route to the Far East?

5 Study picture **A** and read Columbus's account of the meeting.
   (a) Which symbol shows that Columbus would try to convert the natives to 'our Holy Faith'?
   (b) What was that 'Holy Faith'?
   (c) What did Columbus give the natives?
   (d) What did he hope to get in return?
   (e) What evidence is there to show that Columbus could convert by force if he wished to?

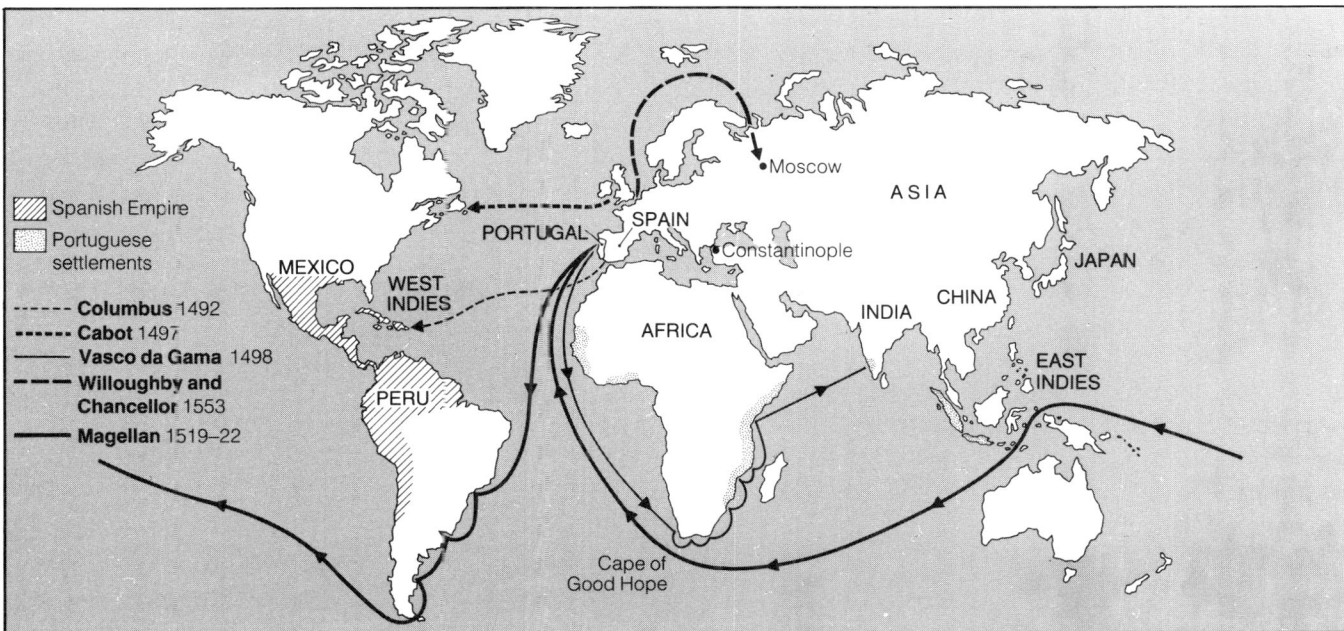

C Exploring new worlds

14 Sir Francis Drake

During the early sixteenth century, Englishmen made voyages of trade and exploration out into the Atlantic Ocean. But they found that the Spaniards and the Portuguese guarded their areas of discovery and settlement.

Spaniards settled in Central and South America, so English people could not set up colonies there. The first English colonies overseas were started on the eastern coastline of North America.

English voyages led to trouble with Spain and sometimes resulted in fighting. John Hawkins traded with Spanish colonies in the New World, carrying black slaves from Africa to sell. He is remembered as one of the founders of the slave trade. In 1567 the Spaniards attacked him and his cousin, Francis Drake, calling them intruders. After that, Drake launched a kind of war against Spanish ships and settlements. *The Spaniards* called him a pirate; *he* believed he was fighting his queen's enemies.

Drake's greatest achievement came between 1577 and 1580 when he set out with five vessels on an expedition. It was supported by several important people, including the queen herself. Some hoped that an English settlement might be made in South America. By the time that

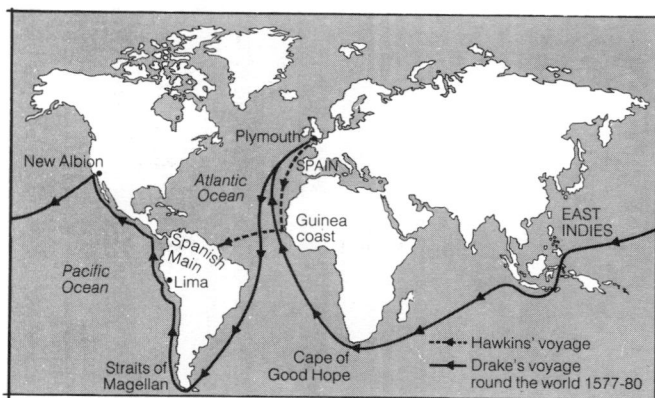

B A portrait of Sir Francis Drake showing also his ship and a map of the world

Drake rounded the south of the continent only one of his vessels remained. He renamed her *Golden Hind* then sailed into the Pacific Ocean, attacking Spanish ships and settlements and capturing great wealth of gold, silver and precious stones.

He then crossed the Pacific to the East Indies where he ran aground but managed to refloat the ship. The ship sailed on to the Cape of Good Hope, where Drake turned north for home.

When the *Golden Hind* arrived off Plymouth in 1580 everyone was amazed, believing that the sailors must have died long before. The news was taken to London, telling of the enormous wealth they had brought back. All the people who had given him money made a good profit.

Drake sailed on to London where the queen visited the ship and knighted him – Sir Francis Drake. He was a public hero in England. However, the Spaniards were angry at the way they had been treated, and war came closer.

A The Elizabethan seamen

Things to do

1. Study map **A** carefully and answer these questions:
   (a) From which port did Drake sail?
   (b) In which direction did Hawkins sail to reach the Spanish Main?
   (c) Through which Straits did Drake pass at the tip of South America?
   (d) How long did it take Drake to sail round the world?
   (e) Which countries opposed Drake and the English?

2. (a) Where did Hawkins sail to?
   (b) Why did the Spaniards call him an intruder?

3. (a) Why did the Spaniards call Drake a pirate?
   (b) Why did Drake believe he was right to attack and rob Spanish settlements?

4. You are an English merchant. Write a letter to your wife explaining to her that you are going to help to pay for Drake's voyage round the world. Use these points: Drake's reputation as a sailor; the Queen's support; new lands to be found; gold, silver, profit.

5. Write a brief entry into the log of the *Golden Hind* just after Drake has been knighted by Queen Elizabeth, summarizing the major events in your voyage around the world.
   or
   Draw a cartoon strip of six scenes showing the most important events in the voyage.

C   John Hawkins

D   **Drake's ship the** *Golden Hind*

E   **Queen Elizabeth knights Francis Drake on board the** *Golden Hind*. **His voyage had captured the public's imagination, opened new trading markets and strengthened England's reputation**

15 The Armada

In the 1580s, relations between England and Spain grew worse. For many years English sailors had raided Spanish ports and ships, trying to capture some of the rich trade with the New World. In 1585, a strong English attack in the West Indies made the Spaniards angry.

Also, England gave help to the Dutch in their fight against Spanish troops. The Earl of Leicester commanded an expedition sent to the Low Countries.

The Pope wished to see England brought back to the Roman Catholic faith, and he encouraged King Philip to launch an attack. Matters were settled by the execution of Mary, Queen of Scots in 1587. Before her death, she made Philip heir to her claim to the English throne.

So a large fleet was prepared in Spanish ports. But in 1587 Drake struck first. He sailed a small fleet to Cadiz and attacked ships there, leaving many ablaze. He called it 'singeing the King of Spain's beard'.

Yet by the following year a new fleet, or armada, was ready. The plan was to sail up the English Channel to the Low Countries, pick up an army there and transport it to invade England. There were 130 ships carrying 8,000 sailors and 18,000 soldiers, under the command of the Duke of Medina Sidonia.

The fleet was sighted off Cornwall on 20 July 1588 and was attacked by English ships for a week. However, by the time they reached Calais, the Spaniards had lost only three vessels.

That night the English floated fireships into Calais harbour and the Armada scattered. Anchors and cables were cut in the panic to escape.

A   **The Spanish Armada**

The next day the wind freshened and the ships of the Armada were driven into the North Sea. The weather worsened as the vessels sailed northwards. English ships sheltered in ports, but the Spanish galleons had no refuge. They were driven on towards the treacherous coasts of Scotland and Ireland.

Some Spaniards landed but were slaughtered by local people. Others perished on rocks in those difficult seas. Crews ran short of food and water. About sixty vessels limped home, many containing dead or dying men. They had failed in their mission.

England was safe from invasion at the cost of less than a hundred sailors killed. Queen Elizabeth ordered a medal to be struck to commemorate her country's escape from danger.

Things to do

1 Copy and complete these statements:

   Reasons for the Spanish Armada sailing to England
   (a) Because for years English sailors —— .
   (b) Because the English attacked —— .
   (c) Because the English helped —— .
   (d) Because the Pope —— .
   (e) Because Mary had made Philip —— .

2 What was 'the singeing of the King of Spain's beard'?

3 (a) Copy map **A**.
   (b) What port did the Armada sail from in Spain?

4 Explain the Spanish plan for the Armada and also explain how the English fleet and the weather destroyed the plan.

5 Conduct an interview between a sailor on one of the English ships and a reporter from local radio. Using all the information in the chapter, write out questions and replies so that the full story of the Armada is told.

Knave

The Pope Consulting with his Cardinalls & Contributing a million of Gold towards the Charge of the Armada.

B A playing card showing a scene from the Armada story

C The Spanish Armada (right) is chased by smaller English ships

16 Tudor everyday life

In Tudor times people ate a main meal in the evening, after the day's work was finished. They liked eating meat – lamb, beef, veal, chicken or rabbit – and had fewer vegetables than we have today. The meat was salted down in barrels for the winter, then cooked on a spit over an open fire.

Poor people had plates made from wood and drank from horn mugs. In richer homes there was pewter ware (pewter is a mixture of tin and lead) and even glass. All people drank ale, beer or cider, with foreign wine if they could afford it. At table they used a knife, a spoon – and their fingers! Forks were seldom seen.

The clothes of ordinary people were made from wool, or a rough cotton called fustian. Some had leather jerkins and cloaks if the weather grew cold. For richer people, however, there were elaborate clothes, especially in Elizabeth's reign. They were cut from fine cloths, felts and silks and were brightly coloured, for men and women alike.

In leisure time people made their own amusements. Singing and dancing were

A The kitchen and dining room in a Tudor house. Notice the furnishings, utensils, equipment, food, servants and family

B The Bear Garden and Globe Theatre on the side of the River Thames.

popular and they liked to watch performances by travelling actors.

They enjoyed sports involving cruelty to animals. Dogs were set to attack bulls or bears. Cock-fighting drew crowds who placed bets on the result. Archery was practised and there were contests with the quarter-staff or with swords, so that men and boys could prepare for war.

In London, theatres were built and plays performed for the public. The greatest playwright of the age was William Shakespeare. His plays could be seen at the Globe Theatre, Southwark, and citizens flocked there. The poorer ones had to stand in the open to watch, and they were called groundlings.

Travel was difficult in those days because there were no proper roads with firm surfaces. Goods were usually carried across the country on the backs of pack-horses. Many people walked on their journeys or travelled on horseback. Coaches were introduced in the middle of the sixteenth century, but only the rich used them. Travelling by road in a coach was very slow.

Things to do

1 Copy and complete these sentences using the words in the Word List.
   (a) In Tudor times people ate —— meat in the —— .
   (b) ——, ——, veal and —— were popular meats.
   (c) People ate a —— meal in the —— .
   (d) Poor people used —— plates and —— mugs.
   (e) All people drank ——, ——, ——, and possibly —— .

   Word List
   lamb   wine   salted   ale   wooden   winter
   horn   main   beer   evening   cider   beef
   rabbit

2 (a) Study picture **A** and describe in detail what you can see in both rooms.
   (b) Is this a rich or poor Tudor home?

3 (a) Study picture **C** and make a list of what you can see at *1, 2, 3, 4, 5* and *6*.
   (b) Which person would not be going to the wedding feast?

4 Copy and complete this grid.

   ## Entertainment

Tudor times	Now
Bull-baiting	Watching TV

5 Imagine you had visited either the Globe Theatre or the Bear Garden (picture **B**). Using the information in the chapter and picture **B** to help you, describe your visit.

C A wedding feast in Tudor times

17 Famous Elizabethans

Elizabeth's reign from 1558 to 1603 produced some of the most famous Englishmen ever. Their work and achievements were so remarkable that they are still remembered today, four centuries later.

Some were 'sea-dogs' who made voyages of exploration and trade. The best-known was Francis Drake, a sturdy ship's captain from Devon who commanded the first English vessel to sail round the world. The Spaniards hated him for attacking their ships and settlements, which they called piracy, but he claimed to be fighting his nation's enemies. He died in 1595 and was buried at sea.

Martin Frobisher in 1576 explored the coasts of Greenland and northern Canada, searching unsuccessfully for a route to the riches of the Far East. Later, John Davis also sailed into the region and explored Arctic waters.

In 1583 Humphrey Gilbert founded a colony on the coast of Newfoundland and four years afterwards his half-brother, Walter Raleigh, tried to start a colony, called Virginia, on the mainland of North America.

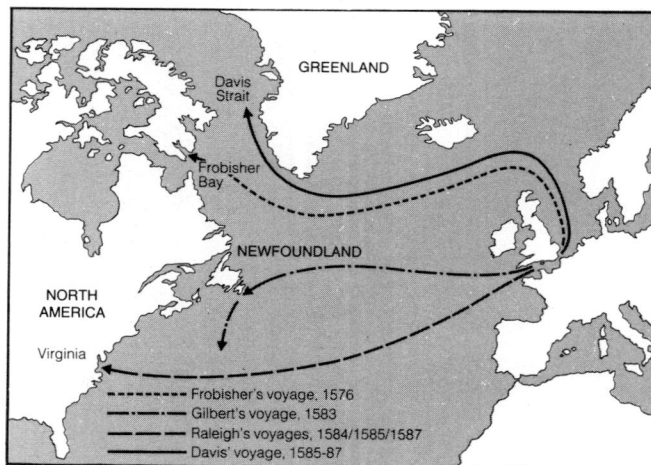

A   **The Elizabethan seamen**

B   **Martin Frobisher and his men fight off Eskimos**

These Tudor sea-dogs encouraged England's great interest in sea trade with lands far away, which has been followed ever since.

The Elizabethan age was also famous for its writers. There were poets and playwrights whose works are still spoken and produced today. Christopher Marlowe, Ben Jonson and John Webster were dramatists whose plays were popular. Some theatres were specially built in London for their performances. The plays appealed to ordinary people, who stood in the open in front of the stage to watch. There were dramas and comedies, tragedies and histories.

The man who wrote the most popular plays was William Shakespeare, born in 1564 at Stratford-on-Avon. When he moved to London his abilities soon became well-known. Shakespeare wrote thirty-seven plays and dozens of poems. They made his audiences happy or sad, proud of their country or thoughtful about greed, jealousy and ambition. These men helped Elizabeth's England to become well-known and respected all over Europe.

Things to do

1 Match up these phrases correctly:

   (a) Elizabeth's reign
   (b) 'Sea-dogs'
   (c) Tudor 'sea-dogs'
   (d) The Elizabethan age
   (e) The greatest playwright

   (i) encouraged great interest in sea trade.
   (ii) was William Shakespeare.
   (iii) was famous for its writers.
   (iv) were sailors who made voyages of discovery.
   (v) produced some of the most famous Englishmen.

2 Explain where each of the following sailed to and what they are remembered for: Frobisher, Gilbert and Raleigh.

3 What dangers do you think sailors at this time might have had to face?

4 List three writers, other than Shakespeare, who were popular in Elizabethan times.

5 Using the information and pictures in this chapter and in chapters 13 and 14, write a summary of the years of exploration and discovery in your own words. Here are some topics to help you get started: trade; search for a new sea route; belief that the world is round; Columbus; Magellan; Drake, and so on.

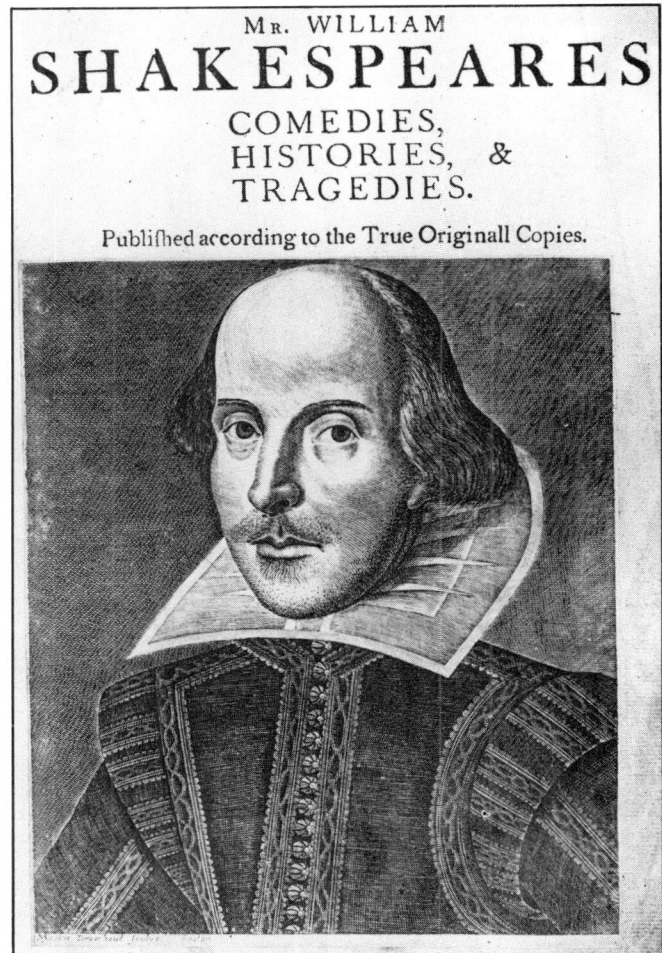

C Sir Walter Raleigh, another famous Elizabethan seaman

D William Shakespeare (1564–1616), whose plays are still performed today

MR. WILLIAM
SHAKESPEARES
COMEDIES,
HISTORIES, &
TRAGEDIES.
Publifhed according to the True Originall Copies.

18 The parish register

Today a careful account of everyone's life is kept by various organizations. Banks, insurance companies and building societies have all sorts of information about people's money. So does the Inspector of Taxes! Details of driving licences and passports are held on computers. Births, deaths and marriages have to be registered in the area where they take place. A great deal can be learned by studying these records.

Parish registers were ordered to be kept from September 1538 by Thomas Cromwell, who carried out much of Henry VIII's policy against the Roman Catholic Church. He ordered that:

'. . . every parson, vicar, or curate within this Diocese [group of parishes], for every Church keep one Book or Register, wherein he shall write the day and year of every Wedding, Christening, and Burial . . . and also there insert every person's name, that shall be so wedded, Christened and buried.'

So from that time the registers were kept, and they give many details of people and their lives in Tudor and Stuart times.

For example, the register of Staplehurst in Kent stated:

B **The parish chest where registers, communion cups and any items made of precious metal were kept**

A **Thomas Cromwell, Henry VIII's secretary, who ordered that records of births, deaths and marriages be kept**

'1560, the vii day of April. There was baptised William, son of William Fant, which child was born in troublous days and therefore not christened till it was a year old.'

Another, in London, showed that road accidents occurred even in Tudor times: 'A Woman, killed by the Lord Windsor's waggon horses, 9th December 1586.' A fine spectacle offered in Loughborough ended in tragedy:

'1579, Roger Shepherd . . . was slain by a lioness which was brought into the town to be seen of such as would give money to see her. He was sore wounded in sundry places and was buried on the 26th day of August.'

The register of St Andrew's, Holborn, shows how illness could strike in an age when little could be done to prevent it:

'1563–4 February: Here, by God's mercy the plague did cease; whereof died in the parish, this year, to the number of four hundred four score and ten.'

You can see how valuable these records are for historians who study Tudor and Stuart times. Try to discover some of the entries for those years in the parish where you live.

Things to do

1. List five types of records kept by the government.

2. (a) Why was September 1538 an important date?
   (b) What did Thomas Cromwell order?
   (c) What effect would this have?

3. Study picture **C** and list some of the names children were given in 1690.

4. Imagine you are a parson in Tudor England. Write an entry in your register about the plague. Remember to date your entry and to say how many people have died.

5. (a) Why was it important for the register to be kept in the parish chest (picture **B**)?
   (b) What other items belonging to the church would have been kept in the chest?

C An extract from the register of baptisms of the church of St Peter and St Paul, Godalming, Surrey for the years 1690–91

19 Schools

For most ordinary people in Tudor times, school education was not important. Boys learned a trade from their fathers, became apprentices with a master, or worked on the land. Girls were considered to be less important. When old enough they often became servants or were taught sewing and caring for the home by their mothers. None of these young people needed to read or write in their work, although some were taught to read from a horn book. This was a flat piece of wood, covered with a piece of transparent horn, which was inscribed with the alphabet.

However, education played an important part in the lives of many other Tudor people. At the time of the Renaissance and the Reformation there was a great interest in learning. New printing presses had come into use in England and there were far more books and pamphlets than there had ever been before. So people wanted to learn everything that books and teachers had to say.

In the sixteenth century many schools were founded. Some still exist – the public schools at Rugby, Uppingham and Harrow, for example, started in the reign of Elizabeth I. These were grammar schools, often established by

B **A horn book with the alphabet and the Lord's Prayer**

individuals, merchants or guilds (groups of craftsmen). They were greatly needed after Henry VIII had closed down the country's monasteries, where many boys had been educated up till then.

At these schools there was sometimes only one master. He taught clever boys Latin, together with a little Greek, Hebrew and arithmetic. The subjects on a modern school timetable would have seemed strange to the Tudors.

Much of the learning was done by heart, with a great deal of translation from and into Latin. School started early in the morning, sometimes at six o'clock! The boys worked long hours, often not finishing until early evening. They studied six days a week and there were very few holidays.

In the days before fountain pens, ball-point pens and pencils they wrote on slates, or on parchment with a sharpened goose feather dipped in ink. Discipline was strict in class. Boys were beaten with a birch by the masters for not learning properly or for bad behaviour.

A **A modern picture of the inside of the grammar school at Stratford-upon-Avon**

Things to do

1 Answer **true** or **false** to these statements:
   (a) Education was not important to most people in Tudor times.
   (b) Boys became apprentices or worked on the land.
   (c) Girls were considered important and had to be educated.
   (d) Girls became servants and did housework.
   (e) Most people could read and write in Tudor times.

2 Draw a picture of a horn book showing the letters of the alphabet.

3 (a) Why was education important to some people?
   (b) Name some schools in existence in Tudor times.
   (c) Why were grammar schools needed?

4 Write out two lists under the headings 'Then' and 'Now' to show the differences between Tudor and modern schools. Use these ideas: subjects, times, equipment, games, holidays, punishment, buildings.

5 Imagine that you taught at one of the schools mentioned in this chapter in Tudor times. Using all the information and pictures, record the events of a day in the school log book.

C Inside a Tudor grammar school. Look carefully at the masters, the boys, the equipment and the punishment

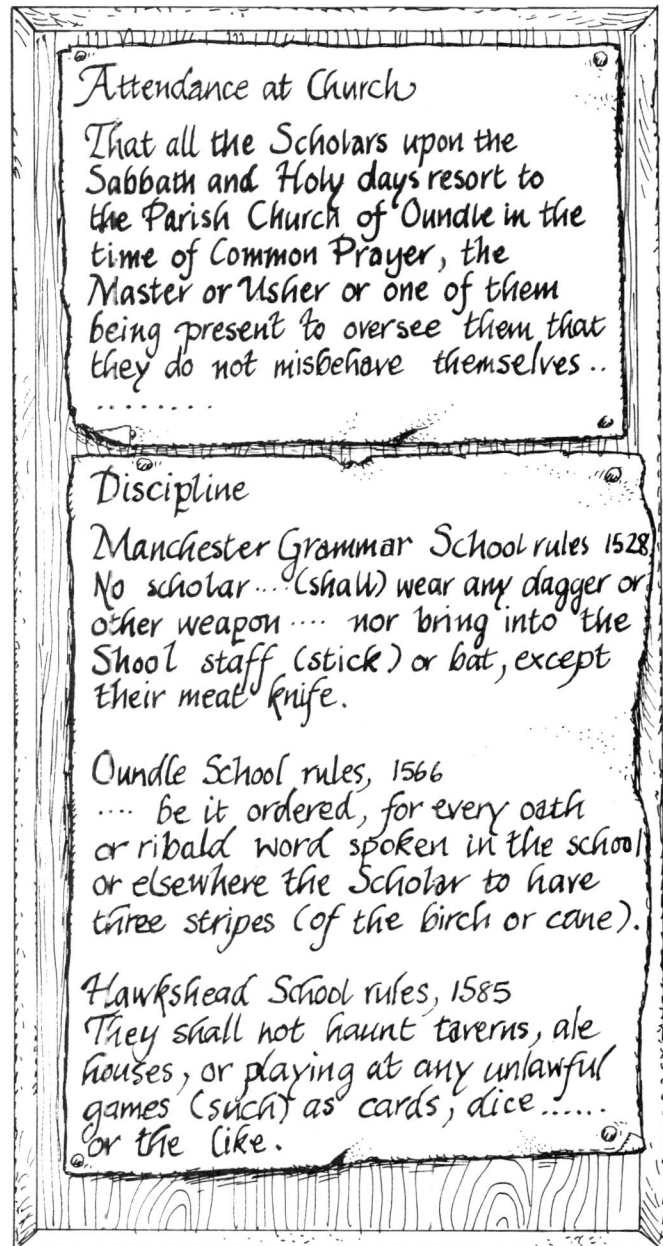

Attendance at Church

That all the Scholars upon the Sabbath and Holy days resort to the Parish Church of Oundle in the time of Common Prayer, the Master or Usher or one of them being present to oversee them that they do not misbehave themselves ..
....

Discipline

Manchester Grammar School rules 1528
No scholar .... (shall) wear any dagger or other weapon .... nor bring into the Shool staff (stick) or bat, except their meat knife.

Oundle School rules, 1566
.... be it ordered, for every oath or ribald word spoken in the school or elsewhere the Scholar to have three stripes (of the birch or cane).

Hawkshead School rules, 1585
They shall not haunt taverns, ale houses, or playing at any unlawful games (such) as cards, dice ......
or the like.

D Examples of school rules in the sixteenth century

20 Town life and houses

In Tudor times there were probably no more than 4,000,000 people in the whole of Britain. Most lived in villages and hamlets dotted across the countryside. Their lives were closely connected with farming, the seasons and the land.

There were not many large towns. The biggest was London, which was a thriving port as well as the capital. It was the most important trading centre in the country. Other large towns included Bristol, Norwich and York, which held markets for people from many miles around. Towns also grew where the wool trade flourished.

London was busy, with hundreds of people jostling in the narrow, cobbled streets. One of its largest buildings was the old St Paul's Cathedral. The great church was used not only for worship, as citizens would gather there to do business or exchange news. Another landmark was London Bridge, with houses and shops built across its length and the heads of executed traitors stuck on poles at one side.

By Elizabeth's reign homes had improved, with more comfort than there had been in the Middle Ages. Most houses had wooden frames and the

A Little Moreton Hall, Cheshire. A fine surviving example of Tudor architecture

spaces were filled with wattle and daub (twigs plastered with mud).

The homes of the rich had wooden floors and wall panelling. There were fireplaces in living-rooms to give heat in the winter. Glass windows were fitted, consisting of many small panes held together by strips of lead.

These houses were built from local materials, such as stone, brick or timber, varying in different parts of Britain. Outside, gardens were planned and planted with care. They contained flowers and shrubs, as well as herbs which were used in cooking and medicine.

Furniture was made from wood and had no padded upholstery. Stools and chairs were not comfortable and people sat at a heavy, carved table in the parlour for their meals. They slept on feather mattresses, which were sometimes laid on four-poster beds.

In those days the lavatory was usually an earth-closet outside and standards of cleanliness were low. Although soap was made, Tudor people were not keen on washing. Some of them would not have a bath more than once a year!

B The kitchen of Bolling Hall, Bradford

Things to do

1 (a) How many people lived in Britain in Tudor times?
  (b) Where did most people live?
  (c) Which was the largest town?
  (d) Why was it so important?
  (e) List three other large towns.

2 Study picture **B**.
  (a) What was the main source of heat?
  (b) What material is used for the floor?
  (c) How would water and food be stored?
  (d) What material would be used for the furniture?
  (e) Would much of the food be home-grown or home-made?

3 If standards of cleanliness were low, what do you think might be the results?

4 Draw a picture of Little Moreton Hall (picture **A**) and underneath it write a few sentences about how it was built and what you might expect to find inside and outside.

5 Using picture **C** and the information in the chapter, *either*:
  (a) write a letter to your family describing your stay in Tudor London; *or*
  (b) prepare a brochure for business people stating the advantages of setting up their business in London.

C London in the sixteenth century. Note all the churches, the bridge (and the skulls on it), the densely-packed houses and the river transport

21 Elizabeth I and her Court

Throughout her reign Elizabeth was loved by her people. In the days before photographs, radio or television, many never saw or heard her. So each year she made several 'progresses', travelling round England. She stayed in one of her palaces, or in large houses, meeting people in towns and villages.

Around the queen were her Court, like a big family. There were advisers such as Lord Burghley and noblemen like the Earl of Leicester, her favourite for many years. Others were bold adventurers like Sir Walter Raleigh. She was always attended by ladies-in-waiting and there were scores of servants.

Elizabeth loved good company, and courtiers were expected to play an instrument, dance and ride a horse. She played the virginals (a keyboard instrument) and enjoyed dancing. At Court, groups of actors performed plays and entertained the company.

In the summer the Court travelled round the country, with the queen riding side-saddle or in a litter. People cheered as she passed. To carry the food and goods needed, hundreds of carts were hired by Elizabeth's officials.

Wherever they were, in London or on a journey, huge quantities of food and supplies were needed by the nobles and servants at Court. In one year they ate over 13,000 lambs, nearly 3,000 chickens and over 4,000,000 eggs. To quench their thirst they drank 600,000 gallons of beer and ale!

The queen lived in great style and loved to receive expensive presents. Feasts were given at Whitehall for hundreds of guests, including foreign princes and ambassadors. She wore expensive dresses decorated with pearls and precious stones and was the centre of attention.

A Queen Elizabeth and her court stag-hunting. The Queen (1) sits alone whilst the court, servants and huntsmen eat and rest

In later years the young Earl of Essex became Elizabeth's favourite courtier. However, he failed in a mission to defeat a rebellion in Ireland and came home in disgrace. To make matters worse, he organized an uprising in England. At last the queen had him beheaded.

Elizabeth was lonely in her later years because so many of her old courtiers had died. She had no children so the best claim to the throne was held by James VI of Scotland, the son of Mary, Queen of Scots.

When she died at Richmond Palace on 24 March 1603, a messenger galloped away with the news. Thirty hours later he arrived in Scotland, to tell James that the crown of England was now his.

Things to do

1 Study picture **A** very carefully then copy and complete these sentences.
   (a) At *1* I can see _____.
   (b) The man at *2* is _____.
   (c) The pages at *3* are _____.
   (d) The men at *4* are _____.
   (e) At *5* a servant holds _____.

2 Copy picture **C** into your book. You may colour your sketches.

3 (a) What were 'progresses'?
   (b) Why did Elizabeth make these 'progresses'?
   (c) Who advised the queen?
   (d) Why did the Court travel with the queen?
   (e) List the food and drink consumed by the Court in one year.

4 Write down (a) some reasons why you would have liked to have been Queen Elizabeth and (b) reasons why you would not like to have been her.

5 In picture **B** you can see Queen Elizabeth's funeral procession.
   (a) How did people in those days learn of such events?
   (b) Write a newspaper article describing the funeral.
   (c) As a political correspondent for the same newspaper write a brief summary of the important events of Elizabeth's reign. (You will have to refer to previous chapters.)

C An Elizabethan nobleman, the Earl of Dorset, wearing the clothes of a rich man. Note the high collar, the doublet (the close-fitting garment on the upper part of his body), padded and embroidered breeches, silk stockings and gloves. His hand rests on his helmet, indicating that he would fight for his country if necessary

B The funeral of Elizabeth I, 28 April 1603. Many people followed her coffin

22 James I

The man who succeeded Elizabeth I in 1603 was already a king. He was James VI of Scotland, the son of Mary, Queen of Scots and her second husband, Lord Darnley. He had been monarch there since 1569, when he was a baby. His mother had fled to England and the crown passed to him. Regents (guardians) were given power to govern until he was old enough to make his own judgements.

James lived through troubled years and three out of his four regents died violently. There were many squabbles among Scottish noblemen, as well as religious quarrels as the Protestant faith grew. The Church became known as the Presbyterian Church.

At the age of thirty-six the new king was a learned man. He had a good education and was clever and quick at book learning. His brain was sharp but in spite of this James was not wise. Someone called him 'the wisest fool in Christendom'. Elizabeth chose well in selecting friends and men to serve the nation. But James lacked wisdom and was a poor judge of character.

So James was never loved by his people as Elizabeth had been. They saw a man with thin legs, a large tongue and untidy clothes. He failed to gain their loyalty. The arrival of the Stuarts on the throne brought a new age to English history.

In his reign James had problems over religion to settle. Catholics, Puritans and members of the Church of England all hoped that the king would show them favour. But James disliked Puritans and Catholics and this brought him trouble.

The king argued with his Parliaments over 'the Divine Right of kings'. It had always been

A   **A picture showing James I**

believed that kings had been appointed by God and therefore their decisions could not be questioned. James was determined that Parliament should not interfere with his wishes.

Parliament had gained more power in Elizabeth's reign and intended to keep it. When the king argued with them over who should make decisions, they refused to give him money, and the quarrel went on for years. James spent money on his Court and his special friends, known as favourites. Because Parliament refused him money in 1614, the king dismissed the members and ruled alone until 1621.

When James died in 1625, all these troubles were passed on to his son, Charles.

Things to do

1 Answer these questions in sentences:
 (a) Who became king of England after Elizabeth?
 (b) Who were the parents of James?
 (c) How long had James been king of Scotland?
 (d) Who governed Scotland whilst James was a boy?
 (e) Who was called 'the wisest fool in Christendom'?

2 Study picture **B** and complete these exercises:
 (a) Name the man.
 (b) Can you name the town?
 (c) Imagine you are a member of the royal Court. Write a letter to your friend in the country comparing James with Elizabeth. Here are some clues: wisdom, judge of character, dress and appearance, popularity.

3 What did the Catholics, Puritans and Church of England expect from James?

B A romantic portrait of James I on horseback. In reality he was not as impressive

4 In picture **C** you can see a picture of James in the House of Lords.
 (a) Explain in your own words what James meant by 'Divine Right of kings'.
 (b) Explain why Parliament opposed this.
 (c) Give examples of the quarrels between James and Parliament.
 (d) Who would you have supported — James or Parliament? Give reasons.

C James I sits in the House of Lords surrounded by bishops and earls. The king argued with Parliament over who should have the most power

23 The Gunpowder Plot

Every year many people take part in celebrating an event which occurred in 1605. They build a bonfire and burn a 'guy'. Fireworks are let off during a kind of party held in November.

When James I became king in 1603, the people of England wondered what line he would take on religious matters. Would he keep the Church of England as it had developed under Elizabeth? Would he help the Puritans who wanted control of the Church taken away from bishops and the ruling classes in England? Would he be more merciful towards Roman Catholics who had been persecuted in the previous reign?

At a conference of Church leaders held in 1604 at Hampton Court he surprised many of those present by showing a wide knowledge of religion as he gave his decision. He said he did not like the Puritans' arguments and he would not make life easier for the Roman Catholics.

Afterwards, a few Catholics decided on a desperate step. Under the leadership of Robert Catesby, they plotted to blow up the House of Lords while the king was there opening Parliament. Then they would capture Prince Charles and Princess Elizabeth, the king's children, put one of them on the throne and restore the Roman Catholic Church to England, with Spanish help.

One plotter, Thomas Percy, rented a cellar under the House of Lords and placed thirty-six barrels of gunpowder there, hidden under bundles of firewood. Guido Fawkes, a Catholic soldier who had served with the Spanish army, offered to light the fuse.

A few days before the opening of Parliament, Lord Monteagle, a Catholic, received a mysterious letter. It warned him not to attend

A James I and his officials ask Guy Fawkes about the Gunpowder Plot. They would want to know who else was involved

because 'They shall receive a terrible blow.' The letter was shown to the authorities who ordered a search of the Parliament buildings.

The plotters left London and Fawkes remained behind. However, on the night of 4 November he was discovered near the gunpowder by guards. After torture he confessed and gave the names of his friends. They were pursued to Worcestershire where some were killed and others captured.

After being tried for treason, all were put to death. Nevertheless some details of the plot remain a mystery. Did the authorities know about the plan beforehand? Was the letter to Monteagle a forgery? Such doubts do not trouble people today when they let off fireworks and burn the guy on 5 November.

Things to do

1 Why do we celebrate bonfire night and burn the guy?

2 What questions about religion did people ask when James I became king in 1603?

3 Look at picture **B** and also read the chapter carefully. Explain what persons 1, 2 and 3 planned to do.

4 Study picture **A**.
   (a) Who is person 1?
   (b) Who is person 2?
   (c) What questions would person 2 ask person 1?
   (d) What answers would person 1 give?
   (e) What happened to person 1?

5 What do you think James and his advisers would do about Catholics after the Gunpowder Plot?

C The execution of the Gunpowder Plotters. After hanging, their bodies were cut up

B The Catholics who planned to blow up Parliament and the king

24 The English in the New World

As the Spaniards settled widely in Central and South America, they built an empire there. They made sure that no other Europeans set up colonies in those regions. This meant that the first English colonies overseas were started during the Tudor age in parts of North America.

Humphrey Gilbert, a half-brother of Sir Walter Raleigh, realized that the eastern coastline of North America was suitable for English settlers. In the period 1578–83 he made several voyages to the New World but on the last one his ship and crew were lost in a wild Atlantic storm.

In 1585 Walter Raleigh organized an expedition which sailed under the command of Sir Richard Grenville. A pioneer settlement was set up on Roanoke Island and was called Virginia. But in the next year all the settlers returned to England. Another colony was also founded on the American coast but its people were probably all slaughtered by Indians. By the end of Elizabeth's reign these settlements had not been a success.

When James I became king more settlements were established in North America. Jamestown in Virginia was founded in 1607.

Then in 1620 came an important event in American history. A group of English Puritans decided to emigrate in their search for religious freedom. A company was formed to finance their scheme and permission was given by the Virginia Company for a settlement to be founded in an area of North Virginia known as New England.

In August 1620, 102 Puritans left Plymouth on the *Mayflower*. After many adventures, having crossed some 5,000 kilometres of wild ocean, they arrived safely off the North American coast

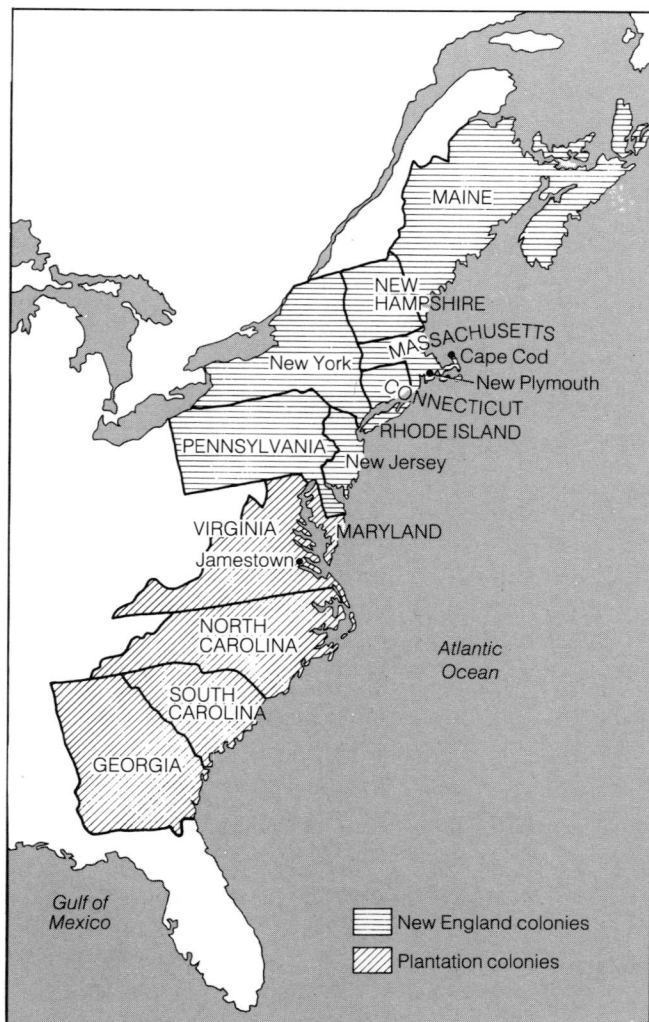

A   **The English colonies in North America**

two months later. The *Mayflower* sailed along the coast until a suitable place for settlement was found. This was called New Plymouth.

The winter was harsh and many settlers died. But gradually they set up a colony, often being helped by the local Red Indians. These Puritans have become well-known in the story of America and they are generally called 'The Pilgrim Fathers'.

Things to do

1 Rearrange the letters to form a name.
   (a) eamAirc
   (b) iVirngai
   (c) sPtunira
   (d) fMlareyow
   (e) ilPFigtehasmrr

2 Why were English colonies set up in North America rather than in Central and South America?

3 Copy map **A** into your book.

4 Explain why the Puritans emigrated to America.

5 Draw a cartoon strip of six scenes to illustrate the journey and settlement of the Pilgrim Fathers. Under each picture write a sentence or phrase to explain your idea. (Ideas: religious freedom; Virginia Company; *Mayflower*; landing in America; building Jamestown; Red Indians.)

B **Portrait of Sir Humphrey Gilbert**

C **An Indian village surrounded by a wooden fence**

D **The *Mayflower* leaving for America. The ship was only 27.5 metres long and 6 metres wide. There were about a hundred passengers**

25 Charles I and Divine Right, 1625 – 40

Charles I's reign between 1625 and 1640 was filled with troubles. The main quarrel was over the rights of the king and the power of Parliament. Who should have the last word in governing the country?

Charles was very different from his father. He was dignified and deeply interested in art and architecture. Yet he was a weak man in many ways, easily led by others. Soon after he came to the throne he married Henrietta Maria, a French princess. She was only fifteen but later had a strong influence on her husband.

But in one respect Charles was similar to his father. He believed in the Divine Right of kings. For the first four years of his reign he argued with Parliament over money. Charles relied heavily on grants which Parliament made to him. But the members would not be generous unless Charles allowed them a bigger say in his plans. For example, they wanted to discuss religious reform and foreign policy. They realized that they could control Charles through cutting his grants.

So in 1628 they refused money until he signed a document which they presented to him. This was the Petition of Right which demanded that taxes should not be collected unless Parliament allowed it and that people should not be imprisoned without trial. The king had to agree to sign.

But in the next year, after further quarrels, Charles dismissed Parliament and ruled without them for eleven years. Two men in particular helped him in that period. One was William Laud, the Archbishop of Canterbury, and the other was Thomas Wentworth, the Earl of Strafford.

Charles's main difficulty was raising money.

Lawyers found old laws which forced loans from the rich and from landowners. The king was using the law for his own ends. In 1637 a well-known Puritan, John Hampden, refused to pay 'Ship Money' which was intended to build up the Royal Navy. In court he lost his case, but many people believed he was right.

In 1640 Archbishop Laud tried to impose his religious ideas on the Scots. However, they objected and their army invaded northern England. This gave Charles a big problem, because he needed money desperately for raising forces to fight them. He realized that he could get it only by recalling Parliament.

A Archbishop Laud, a friend and adviser of Charles. Laud tried to impose his religious ideas on Scotland

Things to do

1 Copy and complete these sentences using the words in the Word List:
   (a) Charles I's reign between —— and 1640 was filled with ——.
   (b) The major quarrel was between the —— and ——.
   (c) The king relied heavily upon —— from Parliament.
   (d) MPs wished to have a bigger say in the ——.
   (e) Parliament could control the —— by cutting his ——.

   Word List
   king grants king troubles king's grants
   1625 Parliament policies

2 Explain why:
   (a) Charles believed in the Divine Right of kings.
   (b) Parliament presented the Petition of Right.
   (c) Charles ruled without Parliament for eleven years.

3 If you were John Hampden, why would you refuse to pay 'Ship Money'?

B A silver medallion to mark the occasion of Charles I's coronation as King of Scotland in 1633

4 Using all the information in the chapter and also picture **C**, write a report or a short play on the recall of Parliament by Charles in November 1640. Refer to these points:
   Charles – needs money, Scottish wars, Scots invaded England.
   MPs – Charles rules without Parliament, uses old laws to get money, now wishes to rely on Parliament; MPs want more say in policy-making.

C King Charles I in Parliament. Charles and Parliament quarrelled over money and control of government

D The marriage of Charles I and Henrietta Maria of France. Charles believed that his power as King was given to him by God

26 The steps leading to war

Because he needed money badly to fight off a Scottish invasion, Charles I recalled Parliament in November 1640. He had governed without them for eleven years so they were in no mood to forgive him. Many of the members were Puritans who strongly opposed the king's ideas and methods. They intended to make him agree to their wishes.

One of their first acts was to get rid of Thomas Wentworth, the Earl of Strafford. They were displeased that while they had been quarrelling with the king, Strafford had been serving him. Therefore a special bill was passed in Parliament by which Strafford was sentenced to death. He was beheaded in May 1641.

John Pym was a Puritan who led the opposition to the king in the House of Commons. After the execution of Strafford he made more attacks on the royal power. The members of Parliament passed Acts to strengthen their own position. The king's courts which had raised money were abolished. Another law said that Parliament could not be dismissed without its own agreement. Then the Puritans tried to bring in a bill to reform the Church.

B The English Civil War began in August 1642. The King raised his standard (flag) in Nottingham and signalled his intention to fight Parliament

Gradually relations between Charles and his Parliament became even worse. At last he decided to arrest five of the leaders because of the trouble they were causing him. He took 400 soldiers and his nephew, Prince Rupert. When they came to the House of Commons, Charles went in alone. He asked where the five members were, but they had been warned of his purpose and had fled. The king left, empty-handed. The members of Parliament were extremely angry because he had dared to march in on them during a debate.

Six days later Charles left London for York. He called on all loyal men to support him. Parliament asked its followers to oppose the king. For several months both sides gathered their forces, which was difficult in an age when travel and the sending of messages was a slow business.

Then, in autumn 1642, the long-awaited war began.

A Charles failed to prevent the execution of the Earl of Strafford by Parliament

Things to do

1 (a) Why did Charles recall Parliament in 1640?
  (b) When had Parliament last met?
  (c) Which group opposed the king's ideas and methods?
  (d) Who can you see in picture **D**?
  (e) What happened to him?

2 In picture **E** you can see John Pym. List three ways in which Pym and his supporters would have angered Charles.

3 Write a newspaper report describing the king's attempt to arrest the MPs. Your headline is 'King Leaves Empty-Handed'.

4 Study picture **B**.
  (a) Where was the King's standard raised in August 1642?
  (b) Whose portrait is on the picture?
  (c) Which towns had Charles already visited?
  (d) Why do you think he visited them?
  (e) What steps was Parliament taking?

C Charles enters the Commons to arrest the five members who opposed him

D Thomas Wentworth, Earl of Strafford, was adviser to Charles I

E John Pym, the leader of Parliamentary opposition to the king

27 The Civil War

A civil war is a terrible experience for a nation, because fathers may fight against their sons and brothers kill each other.

The English Civil War began in autumn 1642 and ended, after several breaks, in 1648. This was one of the most important events in English history. As a result, relations between monarchs and their Parliaments have been different ever since.

The war split the nation. On the king's side were many of the nobility and great landowners. The Church of England and the Catholics supported him because they disliked Puritans. Many ordinary people considered it wrong to rebel against the king.

The Puritans supported Parliament, together with many merchants and traders. Parliament also controlled the Navy, as well as the great city and port of London. Thus they controlled the nation's trade.

In the early stages, the king's forces, known as Royalists or Cavaliers, did well. Their cavalry, under the dashing Prince Rupert, won several battles. But Charles had left London and could not recapture it.

Two things worked against the Royalists. The first was that Oliver Cromwell, a member of Parliament, trained a highly skilled cavalry force, the Ironsides, which won victories. The second was that John Pym persuaded the Scots to help Parliament.

In 1644 the Scots invaded England. Parliamentary forces marched to join them near York, where they met Royalist troops on Marston Moor. Although Prince Rupert's cavalry fought with their usual dash, Cromwell's Ironsides were steadier and won the day.

A   **King Charles on his charger in 1644. Notice his armour and his troops drawn up in the background**

Next, Parliament trained the New Model Army. In the summer of 1645 they won a great victory at Naseby in Northamptonshire. The king's forces never recovered from losing that battle.

After several other defeats Charles surrendered in 1646 and the fighting stopped. Parliament tried to reach an agreement with the king but he never gave up his ideas of Divine Right. He sought help from anyone who was prepared to give him aid. For example, he made a secret agreement with the Scots who had fallen out with Parliament and were willing to invade England.

By 1648 peace still seemed far away.

Things to do

1 When did the Civil War begin and end? What did it do to the nation?

2 Study and copy the maps **C** and **D**. List the supporters for the king in 1642.

3 What were the king's forces known as? Who led their cavalry?

4 List the main reasons why Parliament was successful in the Civil War.

5 (a) Copy map **B** into your book
   (b) If you were the Royalist commander how would you attack?
   (c) If you were the Parliamentary commander how would you resist this and then counter-attack?

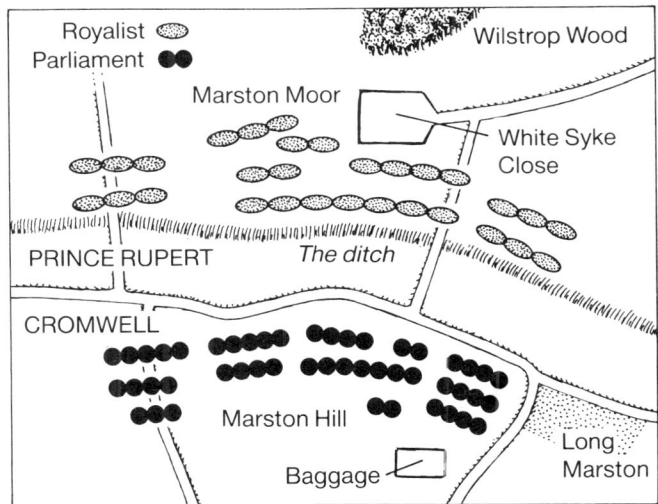

B A plan of the Battle of Marston Moor, Yorkshire, 1644. The battle resulted in a Parliamentary victory

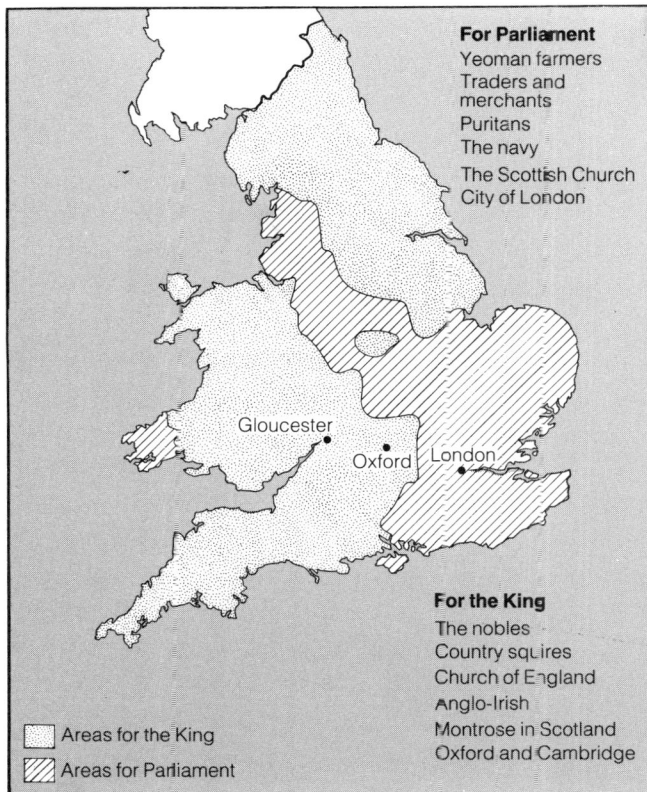

For Parliament
Yeoman farmers
Traders and merchants
Puritans
The navy
The Scottish Church
City of London

For the King
The nobles
Country squires
Church of England
Anglo-Irish
Montrose in Scotland
Oxford and Cambridge

Areas for the King
Areas for Parliament

C England in 1642

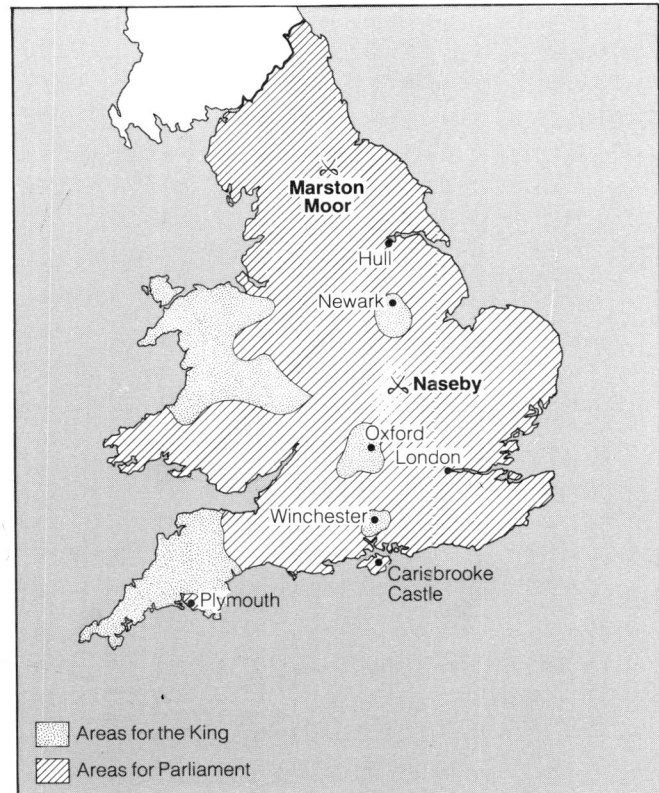

Areas for the King
Areas for Parliament

D England in 1645

28 Trial and execution

Gradually the soldiers of the New Model Army became more powerful in England. They were determined that Charles should be punished for what they considered to be his guilt in starting the war. They claimed he was untrustworthy and always a danger. He never kept his word.

In the summer of 1648 there was a brief outbreak of fighting again, often known as the Second Civil War. Scottish soldiers launched an invasion but were defeated by Cromwell. There were also several uprisings in the south of England by Royalist supporters hoping to help the king. These were put down after bloodthirsty fighting.

A number of Puritan generals believed that Charles should be brought to trial for the sufferings that had been caused to the country. In their view there was only one way to solve the problem – and that was to execute the king. Some members of the House of Commons did not agree but they were not allowed to attend Parliament. Soldiers turned them away at the door.

Thus a trial was arranged. The judges were carefully picked beforehand as men who would find Charles guilty. The king was brought before them at Westminster Hall in December 1648.

He refused to listen to them and claimed they had no right to try him. But the proceedings went on. Charles was called a 'tyrant, traitor, murderer and public enemy'. As the trial came to an end, Charles Stuart, 'man of blood', was sentenced to death.

On 30 January 1649 he was taken to Whitehall. There, on a scaffold in front of a large crowd, he was beheaded. The Civil War was finally at an end. England's king had been killed and his claim passed to his eldest son, Charles.

However, the real rulers of the nation were a group of Puritan army officers who crushed any opposition. One of their number soon became the leader and controlled the others. That was Oliver Cromwell.

A Charles I's death warrant signed by Oliver Cromwell and other prominent leaders of the Parliamentary side

Things to do

1 Read the chapter then copy and complete these sentences:
   (a) The —— became more powerful in England.
   (b) The army thought that —— was guilty of starting the war.
   (c) The King was considered to be ——.
   (d) Cromwell defeated the —— invasion.
   (e) There were —— uprisings in the south.

2 (a) Why did the Puritan generals wish to bring the king to trial?
   (b) What was their solution to the problem?
   (c) What happened to MPs who opposed the generals?

3 Describe the scene you can see in picture **B** and give your opinion on the event *either* as (a) a Royalist *or* (b) a supporter of Parliament.

B A picture showing the execution of Charles I in January 1649. Many people were shocked by this event, others welcomed it

4 Study picture **C** and the chapter (paragraphs 4 and 5).
   (a) Where and when did the trial take place?
   (b) Who is figure *1*?
   (c) What arguments were used against the king?
   (d) What was the sentence?
   (e) Do you think that the judges could have reached another verdict?

C The trial of King Charles I in Westminster Hall in December 1648

29 Oliver Cromwell

Oliver Cromwell was a Puritan country squire from Huntingdon who became a member of Parliament. He was aged forty-three when the Civil War started and soon proved to be a good military leader. By the end of the war he was leader of the army and approved of the execution of Charles.

After that, the Commonwealth was set up. The monarchy and the House of Lords were abolished and the army was left in control. Cromwell led his armies into Ireland and Scotland and won battles there, so that soon he was the most powerful man in the kingdom.

By 1653 he claimed that the members of the House of Commons governed badly, so he replaced them with Army rule. In December 1653 he was made Lord Protector. Cromwell wanted to govern well and was tolerant to many who held different views, yet it was a time of strictness. Some Royalists had their estates seized and harsh Puritan rule made life drab.

From 1655 Cromwell divided England into ten districts, each one under the charge of a Major-General. Laws were passed to restrict what people might do in their everyday lives. Many alehouses were closed; horse-racing, bear-baiting and cock-fighting were banned. Sunday had to be observed strictly as a day of worship and rest. Some English people believed that one tyrant, Charles I, had been replaced by another one, Oliver Cromwell!

Although Cromwell's rule at home was unpopular, he raised England's reputation abroad. War was waged successfully against Spain, both on land and at sea. In the West Indies, Jamaica was captured from the Spaniards and became an English colony. The navy, under the command of Admiral Blake, won several victories.

A A cartoon of 1649 against Cromwell. It shows Cromwell riding on a chariot driven by the devil. Charles I lies under the wheels. Cromwell holds the Church and Liberty on the scales at the end of his sword

The Lord Protector died on 3 September 1658. He had worked hard for what he believed to be right, although some people called him a murderer and a dictator. He was succeeded by his son, Richard. However, the new Protector was not a strong leader like his father, and soon gave up.

England was again faced with the problem of who should rule. At length Parliament decided that one course would be more popular than any other. They would call back Charles, son of the executed king. He had lived abroad since escaping from England in 1651.

Things to do

1 Answer **true** or **false**:
   (a) Oliver Cromwell was a Puritan.
   (b) Cromwell was not a good soldier.
   (c) Cromwell approved of the execution of Charles.
   (d) Cromwell won battles in Ireland and Scotland.
   (e) Cromwell was not very powerful.

2 Study picture **A** and answer these questions:
   (a) Who is riding on the chariot?
   (b) What is the person riding on the chariot holding at the end of his sword?
   (c) Who is under the chariot?
   (d) Who is driving the chariot?
   (e) Explain in your own words what you think the cartoon is trying to say.

3 How did Cromwell and the Major-Generals change English life?

B Oliver Cromwell

4 Study picture **C**.
   (a) What is person *1* saying?
   (b) Why did he say this?
   (c) What does 'This House Is To Lett' mean?
   (d) What did Cromwell become in 1653?
   (e) What did Cromwell want to do?
   (f) Was Cromwell a popular leader?

C Cromwell dismisses the House of Commons for ruling badly in December 1653

30 The Restoration of Charles II

Messages were sent to Charles, son of the king beheaded in 1649, inviting him to return to England and take the throne. At the time, Charles was living in Holland. First he signed a document offering a pardon for most people concerned with the execution of his father. He also promised freedom of worship. A number of Royalists were to be given back their lands, taken by Parliament because they had supported Charles I.

In 1660 he arrived back in England on his thirtieth birthday. Charles was quite different from his father and did not want to fight a long contest with Parliament over who should have the power. He said, 'I do not wish to go on my travels again.'

During the early years of the reign Parliament dealt with the problems of working again with a king. He was given a regular income while the army was paid and disbanded. The Church of England was made the official Church of the country, and Puritans and Quakers (another religious group) were once again treated harshly. This was not what Charles had promised but he could not argue with Parliament.

B Charles II, the 'Merry Monarch', who said he never wanted to go on his travels again

The king wanted people to have more freedom in matters of religion. Secretly he was a Roman Catholic and therefore interested in this freedom. But many members of Parliament opposed this. They did not want Catholics in any position of power. Nor did they want the king to gain the power his father had unsuccessfully fought for.

Charles married a Catholic princess. She was Catherine of Braganza, from Portugal. They had no children, therefore the heir to the throne was James, the king's younger brother. But this caused worry to Protestants, because James was openly a Catholic.

Parliament therefore passed the Exclusion Bill which laid down that no Roman Catholic should be sovereign of England. Charles would not agree. As a secret Catholic he wanted his brother to succeed him.

Towards the end of his reign Charles had a firm position. There had been quarrels over power with Parliament but he had not given way. During his last four years he managed to rule without Parliament.

On his deathbed the 'Merry Monarch' took full membership of the Roman Catholic Church. The crown then passed to his brother, James.

A Charles II in Holland arranging the terms of his restoration to the throne in 1660. He promised a pardon to his father's enemies and freedom to all religious groups

Things to do

1 Look at picture **A**.
   (a) Who is person *1*?
   (b) When did this event take place?
   (c) What did person *1* promise?

2 Describe what you can see in picture **C** using these points: King Charles II; Holland; London; procession; the king's supporters; crowds; end of Puritan rule.

3 What did Charles receive from Parliament?

4 Write a paragraph to explain why Charles and Parliament argued over religion. Use these points: Catholic king; Parliament's fears; the king's brother, James; Protestant fears; Exclusion Bill.

5 Did Charles keep all his promises?

C Charles II rides in triumph through London after returning from Holland. Cheering crowds were glad to see the end of strict and drab Puritan England

D Some of those who agreed to the execution of Charles I were hanged by Charles II. The bodies of Cromwell and some others were dug up

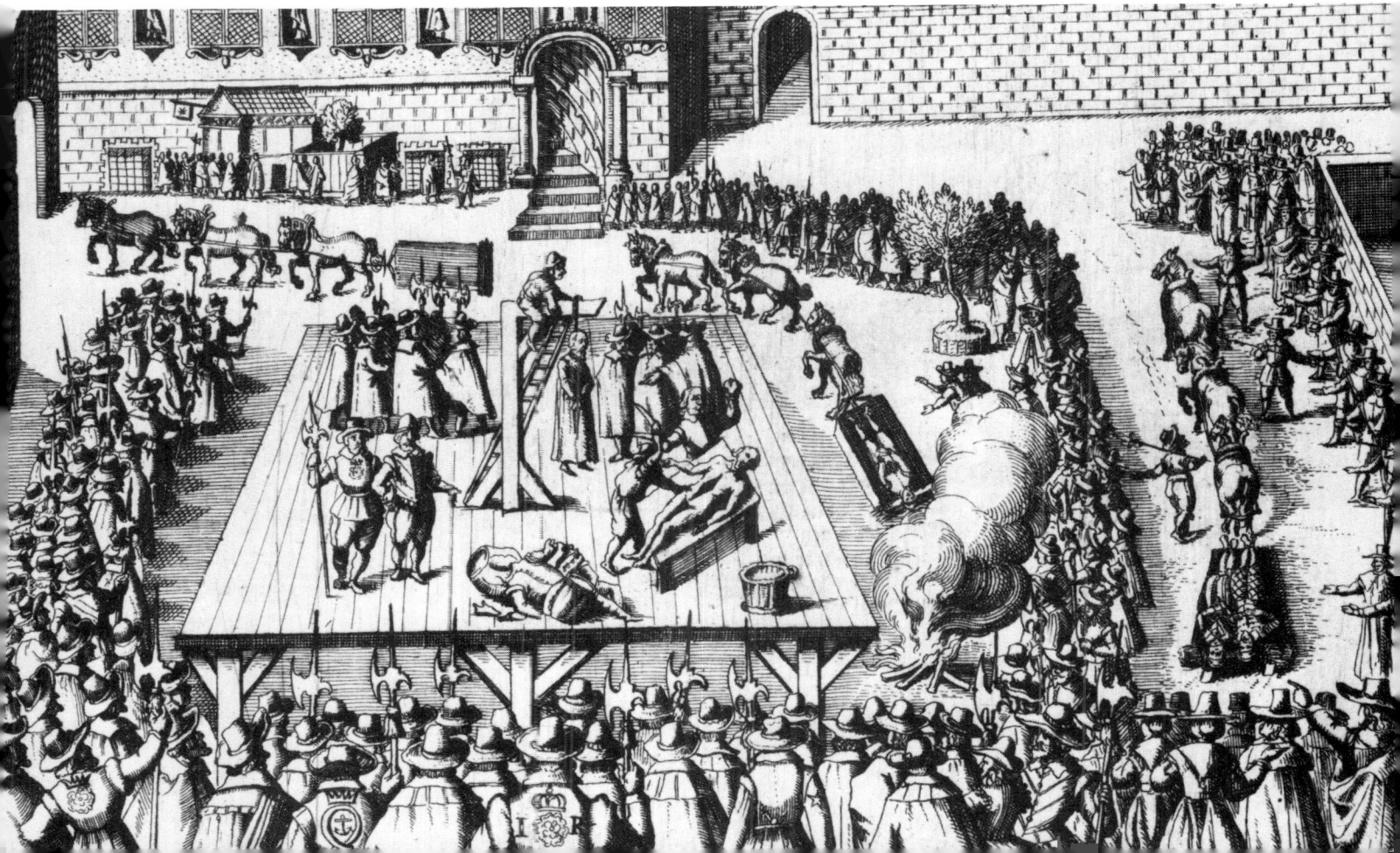

31 The Court of Charles II

By 1660 many English people had come to dislike the harsh rule of the Puritans. Life had become too strict, with laws banning many pleasures. For this reason, there was relief when Charles II came back to the throne.

Charles was an easy-going man. He enjoyed the company of women, liked watching plays at the theatre and was interested in horse-racing. He gathered round him a group of nobles who shared the same interests. They made up his Court and were wealthy lords and ladies.

These people dressed extravagantly and spent great sums of money on clothes and wigs. Both men and women wore very bright colours, in contrast to the Puritans who disliked finery. Gentlemen at Court had brightly coloured waistcoats, edged with lace. Over their shoulders were velvet cloaks, sometimes lined with silk. They wore breeches, silk stockings and buckles on their shoes. They also had ornate hats and carried swords at the waist.

Ladies' dresses had long skirts, made from velvet, satin or silk and were low on the shoulders. They had bright underskirts or petticoats. Often they wore long gauntlet gloves and their hair hung down in bunches of curls.

The Court's centre in London was at the palace of Whitehall, which included the king's residence and many government office buildings. The palace was a vast area covering over twenty acres and containing 2,000 rooms. From this place much of the government of England was carried on.

Charles II often gave the impression of not caring about work and appeared to be lazy. He was a tall man, dark-haired, who described himself as ugly. Although he had no children

A Nell Gwynne

from his wife, Catherine of Braganza, a Portugese princess, he had nine from his mistresses. Two of these were born to Nell Gwynne.

Nell Gwynne was an orange-seller at the King's Theatre. Later she became an actress, when she caught the eye of the king. He bought her a house next door to St James's Palace, where she lived until her death.

At Court, plays called masques were performed, with some acting and some mime. Also, gambling and card playing were popular among a group of people who cared mostly for pleasure and for gaining a high position for themselves.

Charles certainly deserved to be known as the 'Merry Monarch'.

Things to do

1 Copy and complete these sentences by referring to the chapter.
   (a) By 1660 many people disliked _____.
   (b) Life had become _____.
   (c) Charles II was welcomed _____
   (d) Charles II was an _____.
   (e) Charles II enjoyed _____.

2 (a) Copy picture **B** into your book.
   (b) Copy picture **C** into your book.

3 (a) Where was the centre of Charles II's Court?
   (b) Why would people wish to be part of the king's Court?
   (c) What did people do at Court?

4 Who was Nell Gwynne?

B A lady and gentleman in court dress

5 Give reasons why Charles was known as the 'Merry Monarch'. How do you think a king or queen should behave?

C Fashionable London. This is Burlington House, Piccadilly. Notice the gardens, fields and house

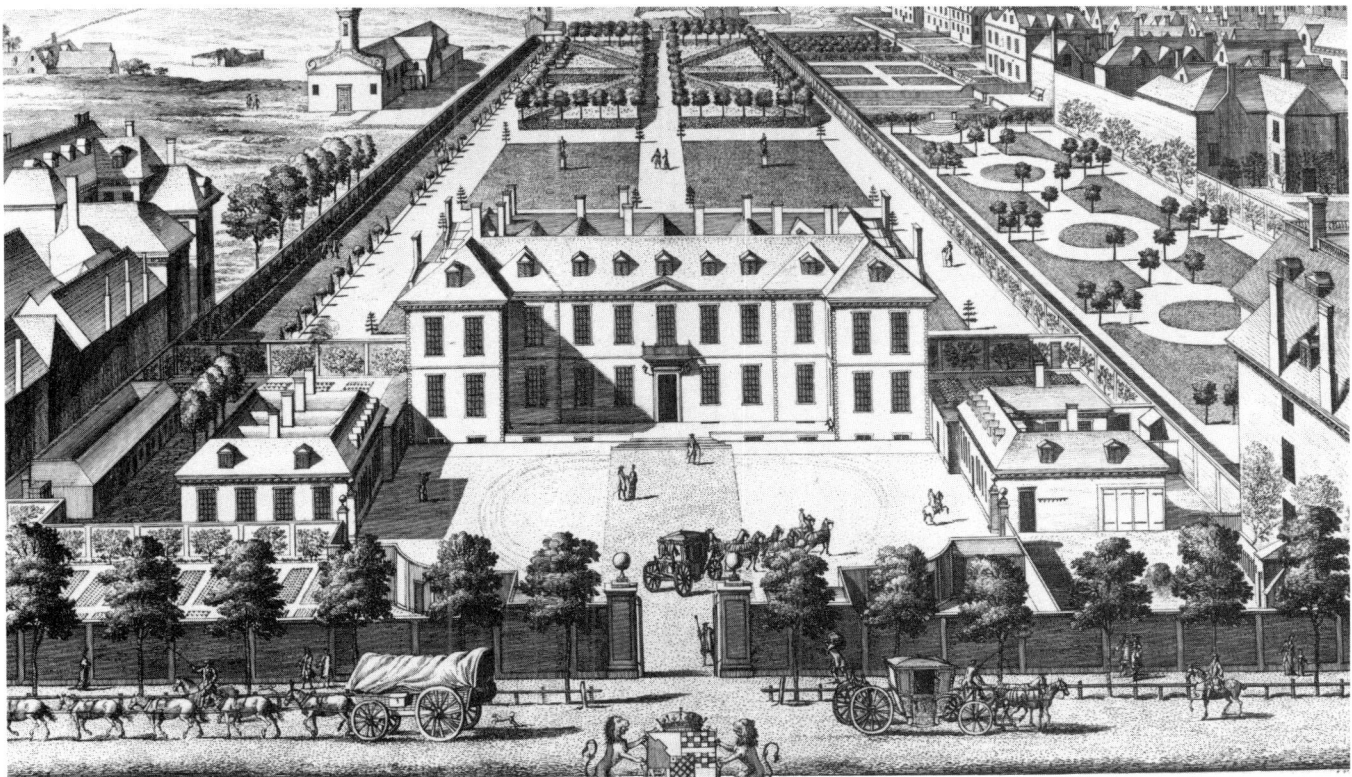

32 The Plague

A terrible disaster hit England early in the reign of Charles II. It is usually known as the Great Plague.

There had been outbreaks of plague for hundreds of years. The general standard of health was poor and illnesses of that type were far more common than they are today. Earlier in the seventeenth century thousands of people had been killed by plagues which swept through the houses and streets of crowded towns where there were no drainage systems or pure water supplies. Therefore no one was surprised when there was an outbreak during the hot summer of 1665.

Probably the disease was bubonic plague, carried in ships bringing cargoes from distant lands. The plague was spread by rats and the fleas living on them. Flea bites on humans led to fever and vomiting, followed by the growth of large black lumps, known as buboes. These lumps appeared under the armpits or in the groin. Death usually occurred within a short time.

Local authorities ordered that any houses containing plague victims should be shut up. A red cross had to be painted on the door, with the message, 'Lord have mercy upon us'. Nobody was allowed in or out of the house. Sometimes victims were taken to a 'pest-house', but often they died at home.

So many died that individual burials and services were impossible. Large pits were dug to take hundreds of bodies which were collected in horse-drawn carts at night.

The severe illness was widespread, there were few doctors and people had little knowledge of disease and medicine. Many streamed out of London into the countryside, but they were not welcomed there.

A A London Bill of Mortality (list of deaths) for the week 15–22 August 1665

Fires were lit in the streets to purify the air, domestic pets were killed and public meetings were banned. Yet the plague continued.

Life in the capital came almost to a standstill and grass grew in the streets. It was not until the coming of the coldness of winter that illness and the death-rate slowed down.

Plague deaths in London	
1603	33,347
1625	41,313
1636	10,400
1665	68,596

Things to do

1(a) If you had been alive in the summer of 1665, would you have been surprised by the outbreak of plague? Give reasons for your answer.

(b) If you were a doctor, how would you recognize plague symptoms?

2 Draw a graph or a diagram to show the number of plague deaths in London in 1603, 1625, 1636 and 1665.

3 Study picture **A**.
(a) How many people had died of plague during the week 15–22 August 1665?
(b) How many parishes were infected by plague?
(c) How many parishes were clear of plague?
(d) What were the other most common causes of death?

4 Study picture **B**.
(a) What measures did people take to avoid the plague?
(b) What job did the 'searchers' do?
(c) Why did a man ring a bell in front of the coffin?
(d) How were plague victims buried?
(e) Why were funeral services impossible?

5 Study picture C.
(a) Why do some of the houses have crosses painted on them?
(b) Why has a fire been lit in the middle of the street?

Multituds flying from London by water in boats & barges.

Flying by land.

Burying the dead with a bell before them.   Searchers.

Carts full of dead to bury.

B Scenes during the Great Plague of 1665

C London during the plague. Notice the writing on the doors, the fire in the street, the man holding a bell

33 The Fire

The summer of 1666 was hot and dry and there were more victims of the plague. But as the summer came to an end another terrible tragedy occurred. In the early morning of 2 September a small fire broke out in London, which was the kind of event that often happened in an overcrowded city. Starting in a baker's shop in Pudding Lane, near the Tower, it soon swept through nearby houses and shops, gaining a strong hold.

A big fire has enormous power which is very difficult to stop. Even today when modern fire engines, turntable ladders and high-pressure pumps are available, it is sometimes impossible to control the flames. In 1666 it was hopeless, because there was no organized fire brigade or machinery.

A strong east wind fanned the blaze. It swept through timber houses which were packed close together, high over narrow streets. Sparks floated across to churches, shops and nearby streets where fresh outbreaks quickly gained a hold. Efforts were made to pull thatch from roofs, using poles, and to throw water on the flames from leather buckets. In some places lines of houses were blown up, to make gaps and stop the fire. But it continued to lick its way across the city.

When they realized the size of the fire, thousands of people started to flock out of London. Some went by road, piling their household goods and treasures on to carts and waggons and heading for the country. Many went in small boats along the Thames, which was an important passenger route in those days.

Much of what we know about the fire comes from the diary of Samuel Pepys who was Secretary of the Navy at the time. He kept a daily account of happenings. He described how

the king himself and his brother, the Duke of York, tried to find ways of stopping the fire.

The fire burned for four days. In that time about 13,000 houses were destroyed. About ninety churches had also been burned, including the famous old St Paul's Cathedral. The damage was enormous, although only six people died.

However, there was one benefit. Many of the packed streets and alleys where the plague had raged were destroyed. The plague was burned up by the fire.

One great task remained – to rebuild the city of London. The government soon began its search for an architect who could do this.

A   **A map made after the fire, showing the centre of London devastated by the flames**

Things to do

1 Read the chapter then copy and complete these sentences:
   (a) On 2 September 1666, a fire broke out in ——.
   (b) The —— started in a —— shop.
   (c) A strong —— fanned the ——.
   (d) The fire soon swept through the —— buildings.
   (e) There was no organized ——.

2 List the ways in which Londoners tried to fight the fire, for example, blowing up houses.

3 Look at picture **B** and using this and other information in the chapter write entries in your diary for 2 and 3 September 1666. Use these ideas: fire starts, fire spreads, people try to escape, people take valuables, the river is safe.

4 Study picture **C**. Do you think that methods such as this would have been effective?

5 Copy and complete this grid:

The Great Fire

The damage	The advantages
Six deaths	Old streets cleared

B The Great Fire of London, painted by a contemporary artist

C Firemen in 1666. Compare this with a modern fire-fighting scene

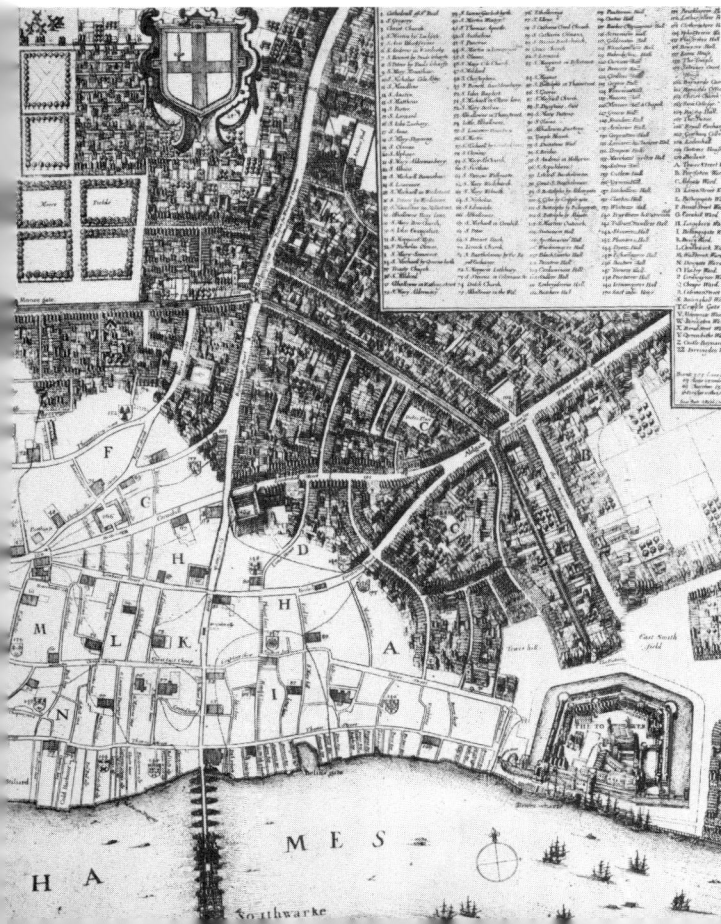

34 The Dutch

During the sixteenth and early seventeenth centuries, English ships were to be seen on many of the world's oceans. Some were on voyages of exploration, others seeking trade. There were good profits to be made by merchants buying and selling goods overseas.

Yet by the middle of the seventeenth century, the English had a great rival at sea. The Dutch were fine sailors and their vessels also sailed the oceans, trading and exploring. They settled in the Spice Islands – the East Indies – and traded there, making their country rich.

Before long there were quarrels among European merchants over their shares of the trade. This led to war between England and Holland in the 1660s.

Fighting began in 1665 and both sides had victories and defeats. However, the Royal Navy had a difficult time. There had been a shortage of money for some years and several vessels were laid up in port. Also some English sailors were not receiving regular pay and a number had actually deserted and gone to fight for the Dutch.

A The Dutch explorer, William Barents, made three attempts to find the north-east passage to India

Therefore in June 1667 the Dutch Admiral, de Ruyter, sailed a fleet to attack English ships. His vessels came right into the River Medway at Chatham where an English fleet was laid up, protected by a large boom (barrier) laid across the river.

The authorities believed that this barrier, covered by guns mounted on shore in the castle, would keep the Dutch out. Yet Admiral de Ruyter's ships sailed in close and bombarded Chatham. They broke the boom and set fire to three English ships, *The Royal James*, *Oake* and *London*. Then they boarded and towed away *The Royal Charles* which was the biggest vessel the Royal Navy possessed. The ship was taken to Holland.

The news of what had happened came as a shock to English people. Their pride was hurt and people blamed the king for spending too much money on his Court instead of defending the country.

The Dutch could not follow up their victory, and later in 1667 the two countries made peace. Nevertheless some men and women looked back to the days when Oliver Cromwell had controlled the country. Those had been times of victory, not defeat, and such a thing would not have been allowed to happen then.

Things to do

1 Study picture **A** and the first two paragraphs of this chapter and answer these questions.
   (a) Where have the sailors come from?
   (b) Where did they settle?
   (c) Give reasons why the Dutch looked for land.
   (d) Draw simple sketches of a European ship and an Indian ship.

2 Why did the Dutch and the English quarrel?

3 Study picture **B** and complete these exercises.
   (a) Name the Dutch admiral 1.
   (b) Where did the battle take place?
   (c) Name four English ships captured by the Dutch.

4 Design the front page of the *Chatham Observer* for 15 June 1667, reporting on the Battle of the Medway. (Use the pictures and the information in the chapter to help you.)

B The English and Dutch fleets in battle in the River Medway. The English defeat was a great shock to the nation

5 From the picture of Amsterdam (picture **C**), draw a simple sketch map. On your map show how you would get from the harbour mouth to the church *1* by canal.

C Amsterdam in the seventeenth century. It was the chief port and commercial centre of Holland

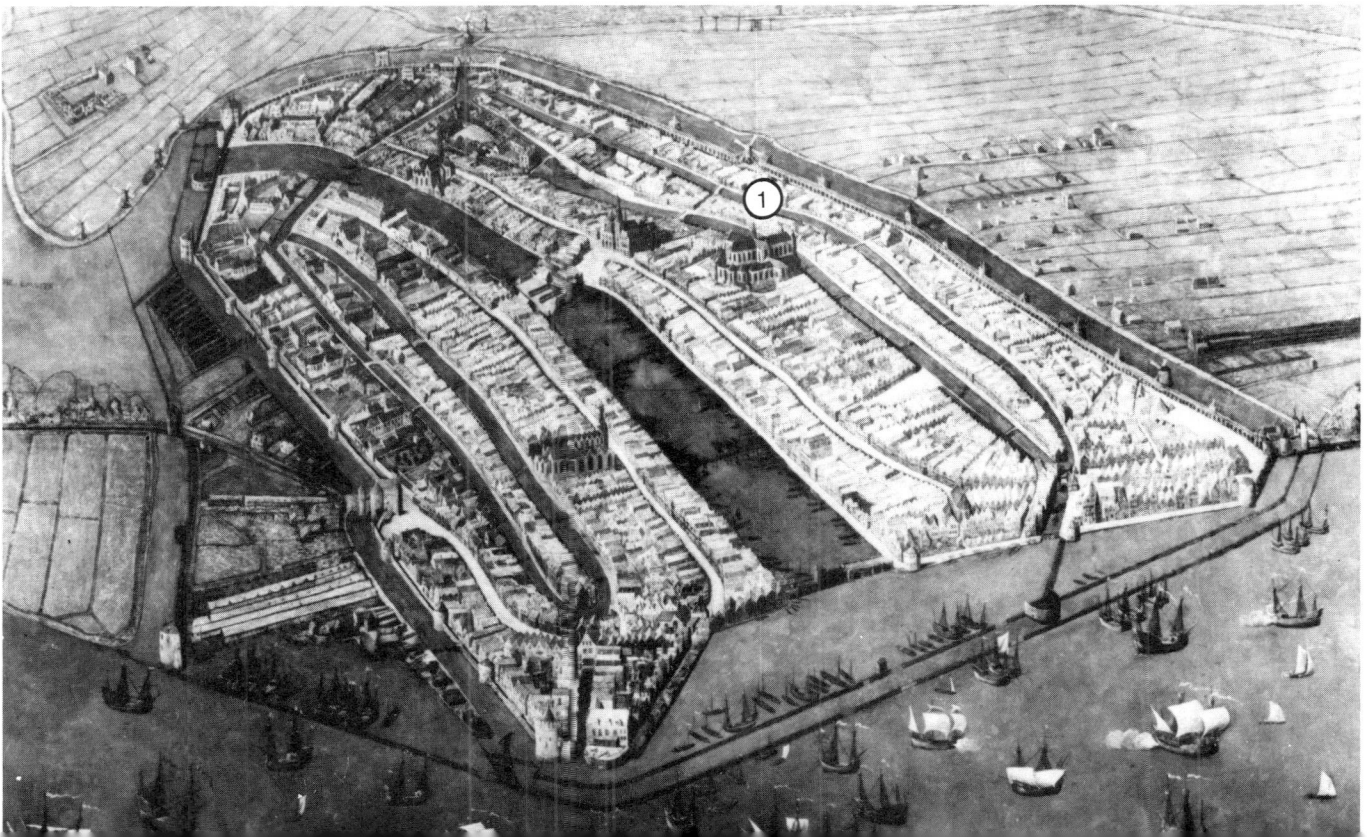

35 Sir Christopher Wren

The Great Fire of London left the authorities with a huge problem. How could they replace the hundreds of destroyed buildings? To plan and supervise the work they chose the person who is generally considered to have been England's most famous architect. His name was Christopher Wren.

Wren was born in 1632, the son of a clergyman. At school he was clever and, when seventeen, went to Oxford University. He had many interests but the main one was astronomy. After making special studies of the moon and of Saturn he became a professor of astronomy.

His interest in architecture started when he designed a chapel at Pembroke College, Cambridge. Then he designed the Sheldonian Theatre at Oxford, where important ceremonies are still held. Wren visited France in 1665 and saw some of the magnificent buildings put up for Louis XIV. He was very impressed and wanted to build in the same style.

On returning to England, Wren prepared a scheme to remodel St Paul's Cathedral which was a giant medieval building. However, shortly afterwards the Great Fire burned it down, so plans were needed for rebuilding. Just four days after the Fire had finished, Wren submitted schemes for replanning London. Much of the plan was never used but he was given the chance to replace the cathedral and city churches.

In 1670 he was appointed Surveyor of His Majesty's Works. This gave him offices in Scotland Yard, a large house and an income for life. He began to plan a giant cathedral and the building went on for many years, from 1675 to 1711. Above it he placed no spire or tower, but the great dome which still stands. The work was a masterpiece.

A   The interior of St Bride's, Fleet Street, London. This was one of Wren's fifty-one new parish churches

In addition Wren rebuilt fifty-one out of the eighty-seven parish churches destroyed in the City of London. Also he worked on other buildings: hospitals, libraries and palaces in several parts of England.

Christopher Wren liked nothing better than drinking in a coffee house with friends, and smoking his pipe. He was knighted in 1675 and lived on to die peacefully in his sleep at the age of ninety.

Few people have left so much work that can still be seen and admired.

Things to do

1. Read the chapter then complete these statements:
   (a) Wren was born in _____.
   (b) In 1649 Wren went to _____.
   (c) Wren visited France in _____.
   (d) In 1670 Wren was appointed _____.
   (e) Wren died at the age of _____.

2. Look at picture **A** and write a few sentences to say what you like or dislike about the design of St Bride's.

3. Name two buildings, other than St Paul's, built by Wren.

4. Study picture **B** and re-read the chapter.
   (a) Who is the man?
   (b) Which cathedral is shown on the plan?
   (c) Why was a new cathedral needed?
   (d) How many churches did Wren build?
   (e) How long did it take to rebuild St Paul's?

5. Choose one important building (airport, town hall, railway station, library) near your house. Draw some sketches of it from memory.

B Sir Christopher Wren. The Great Fire of London gave him the chance to show his architectural skill

36 Science

Today we are in a scientific age. Scientists are important people whose inventions and ideas have altered the way we live. Among other things, they have brought great changes to medicine, travel, industry and farming.

However, before the seventeenth century little was known about science. Some scholars who had ideas different from those taught by the Church could be in trouble if they spoke their opinions publicly. For example, Galileo in Italy believed that the earth and other planets revolve round the sun. The Roman Catholic Church would not accept this teaching, so Galileo had to appear before a committee of churchmen and confess that he was wrong.

In England, Francis Bacon was the Lord Chancellor in James I's reign. He said that nature and science should be studied carefully. In his opinion scientific experiments should be carried out so that more could be learned about the world.

In 1628 William Harvey, who had studied under Galileo, published a book explaining how blood circulates round the body, being pumped by the heart. This was a great step forward in medical knowledge.

The most famous scientist of the time was Isaac Newton (1642 – 1727). He became professor of mathematics at Cambridge and was interested in astronomy. Newton developed the reflecting telescope for studying the heavens. He studied light and also the way that things move. He worked out the law of gravity, probably after watching an apple fall from a tree. Much modern science is based on the methods and laws that he laid down.

Newton was a member of the Royal Society, which was founded in 1662 with the

A Francis Bacon (1561–1620) stressed the importance of experiments and scientific methods

encouragement of Charles II. A group of enthusiastic scientists met together for discussion and learned from each other. Among the members were William Harvey, Samuel Pepys, John Locke, who studied politics, Christopher Wren and Robert Boyle, who had a great interest in chemistry.

Another interesting scientist of the Stuart age was Edmund Halley, a mathematician and astronomer. In 1682 he described the comet which was later named after him and also predicted correctly that it would return in seventy-seven years' time. At the end of the Stuart age he was the first to suggest that the seas are made salt by deposits from rivers that run into them.

Things to do

1 Copy and complete these statements:
   (a) Galileo believed that the earth _____ .
   (b) Francis Bacon said that _____ .
   (c) William Harvey explained _____ .
   (d) Isaac Newton worked out the _____ .
   (e) Edmund Halley described and predicted the _____ .

2 What problem did Galileo face when he tried to explain his theory about the planets?

3 Give four reasons why Isaac Newton is considered to be such an important scientist.

4 Study picture **D**.
   (a) Which king is shown?
   (b) Name the Society of which the king was patron.
   (c) When was the Society formed?
   (d) Name four members of the Society.
   (e) Identify three instruments shown in the picture and say what they might be used for.

C Isaac Newton (1642–1727), the genius who revolutionized science

5 Explain how each of the following inventions or scientific developments has affected modern society: television, space travel, the computer, organ transplants.

B William Harvey (1578–1657) studied at Cambridge and Padua. His discovery of how blood circulates round the body advanced medical knowledge

D A picture showing King Charles II being crowned as patron of the Royal Society. Notice the scientific instruments in the background – set squares, telescopes, a pendulum, scales

37 Everyday life

In the seventeenth century most people lived in villages and hamlets. Life was a constant round of hard work for everyone. They depended on their crops, for any period of drought or flooding could lead to famine and hundreds of deaths from starvation or malnutrition.

Most farming was still carried out under the open field system, where villagers worked on strips of land near their homes. They grew rye or wheat and barley and left a field fallow (resting) one year in three. Some people planted a new crop in their gardens. This was the potato which had been introduced from America at the end of the previous century. Cabbages and carrots, celery and turnips were also grown.

Breakfast was usually taken early, between six and seven a.m. People ate cheese or cold meat and drank ale or beer. The main meal of the day was eaten after work and the usual foods were salt meat, bacon, bean soups, bread and cheese, washed down with beer.

In the village the parson was an important man, and people attended church or chapel regularly. For many, the only book they saw in their lives was the Bible. Yet they could be frightened by superstition. Any old woman in a village might be accused of witchcraft if a neighbour fell ill or had an accident. She would be given a trial and, if found guilty, put to death.

There were many sports and pastimes for people's leisure. Morris dancing was popular and crowds would gather to watch. Football was played, sometimes as a contest between two villages with most of the inhabitants taking part! Children enjoyed many games which have changed little over the centuries. These included marbles, hop-scotch, leap-frog and balancing on a see-saw.

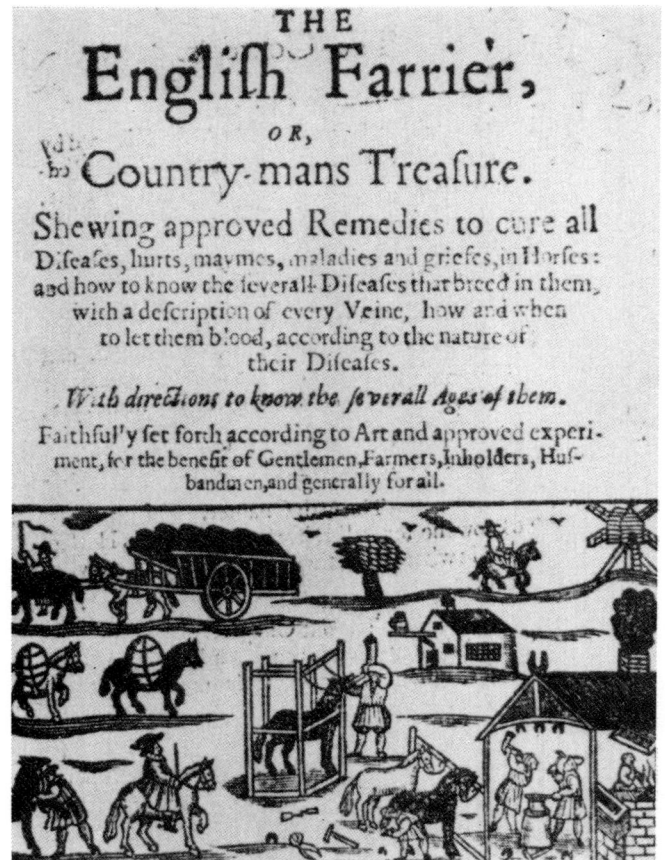

THE English Farrier,
OR,
Country-mans Treasure.

Shewing approved Remedies to cure all Diseases, hurts, maymes, maladies and griefes, in Horses: and how to know the severall Diseases that breed in them, with a description of every Veine, how and when to let them blood, according to the nature of their Diseases.

With directions to know the severall Ages of them.

Faithfully set forth according to Art and approved experiment, for the benefit of Gentlemen, Farmers, Inholders, Husbandmen, and generally for all.

A The front page from a handbook on the care of horses, published in 1636

As in Tudor times, sport involving cruelty to animals was popular. London had its bear-garden where people would lay wagers on bull- and bear-baiting, cock- and dog-fighting, even horse-baiting.

Ordinary people often made their own clothes after weaving the cloth. Women's dresses, worn over petticoats, were made of wool. Working men had rough shirts and woollen breeches.

For all people, life was simple compared with today's.

Things to do

1 Study picture **A**.
  (a) When was the book published?
  (b) Which animal did the book refer to?
  (c) List three ways in which the horse was used.
  (d) How are the men caring for the horses?
  (e) Why were horses so important in those days?

2 Explain carefully:
  (a) what might lead to starvation or malnutrition;
  (b) what the open field system was;
  (c) why someone might be accused of witchcraft;
  (d) what might happen to people accused of wrong-doing;
  (e) why the parson was an important man.

C A tradesman's wife

B A woman accused of witchcraft is given a trial by water. If she sank, she would be considered innocent (but as she would probably have drowned by the time this decision was reached, it wouldn't do her much good!). If she floated, she would be considered a witch and would then be put to death

3 Write out a timetable for a normal day in your life. Give examples of what you might eat at your meals. Alongside your timetable write in the jobs that a young person in Stuart times might be doing and what he or she would be having to eat.

4 Copy and complete this grid. (You will have a longer 'Modern' list.)

Sports and Pastimes

Stuart times	Modern times
Football	Soccer
Marbles	Marbles

and so on

5 Draw examples of Stuart and modern clothes. Write a few sentences under your sketches about the materials used then and now, the styles, and how you would buy such garments.

77

38 Stuart towns

In Stuart times most people in England lived in the south, the midlands and the east of the country. The great cities of the north had not then started to develop and were only small towns or villages.

London was by far the largest place. By the middle of the seventeenth century the population of the capital stood at 250,000 which made it ten times larger than the next biggest town. London was the chief port and trading city, as well as being the centre of government. The number of buildings there had grown since Tudor times, with more brick and stone used in their construction. Yet many of the cobbled lanes and alleys, overhung by houses and shops, had barely changed since the Middle Ages. Dirt, smells and noise were everywhere in the streets.

In the sixteenth century there had been open spaces and houses with large gardens. But by Stuart times many had been filled up by buildings as the population grew.

Hawkers walked round the streets shouting their wares. They sold such items as coal and fruit, ribbons and water. Craftsmen made goods in their shops and sold them from an open room at the front. People wandered along the streets, watching the saddler or the tailor, the shoemaker or the baker at work.

Another important city lay on the western side of Britain. This was Bristol. As trade developed with the American colonies in the seventeenth century, Bristol became a flourishing port, second only to London. Ships and barges there were busy with cargoes from the New World. In particular these included sugar and tobacco.

In large towns coffee houses grew popular. Men would go there to smoke their pipes and chat to friends. They would read a newspaper and talk politics as they drank coffee. Two other drinks which became popular, though they were expensive, were tea and chocolate.

Night-time in towns could bring trouble and danger in the days before there were any police. Groups of wild young men might emerge from taverns, perhaps breaking lamps or rousing citizens from their sleep by knocking on their doors. Travellers in the streets at night would hire a 'link-boy' to carry a flaming torch and guide them home. Such travellers would wear a sword or carry a cudgel (a heavy club) for protection.

A   **Bristol, the second most important city in the country – 'a large city, of great trade, the streets very narrow'**

Things to do

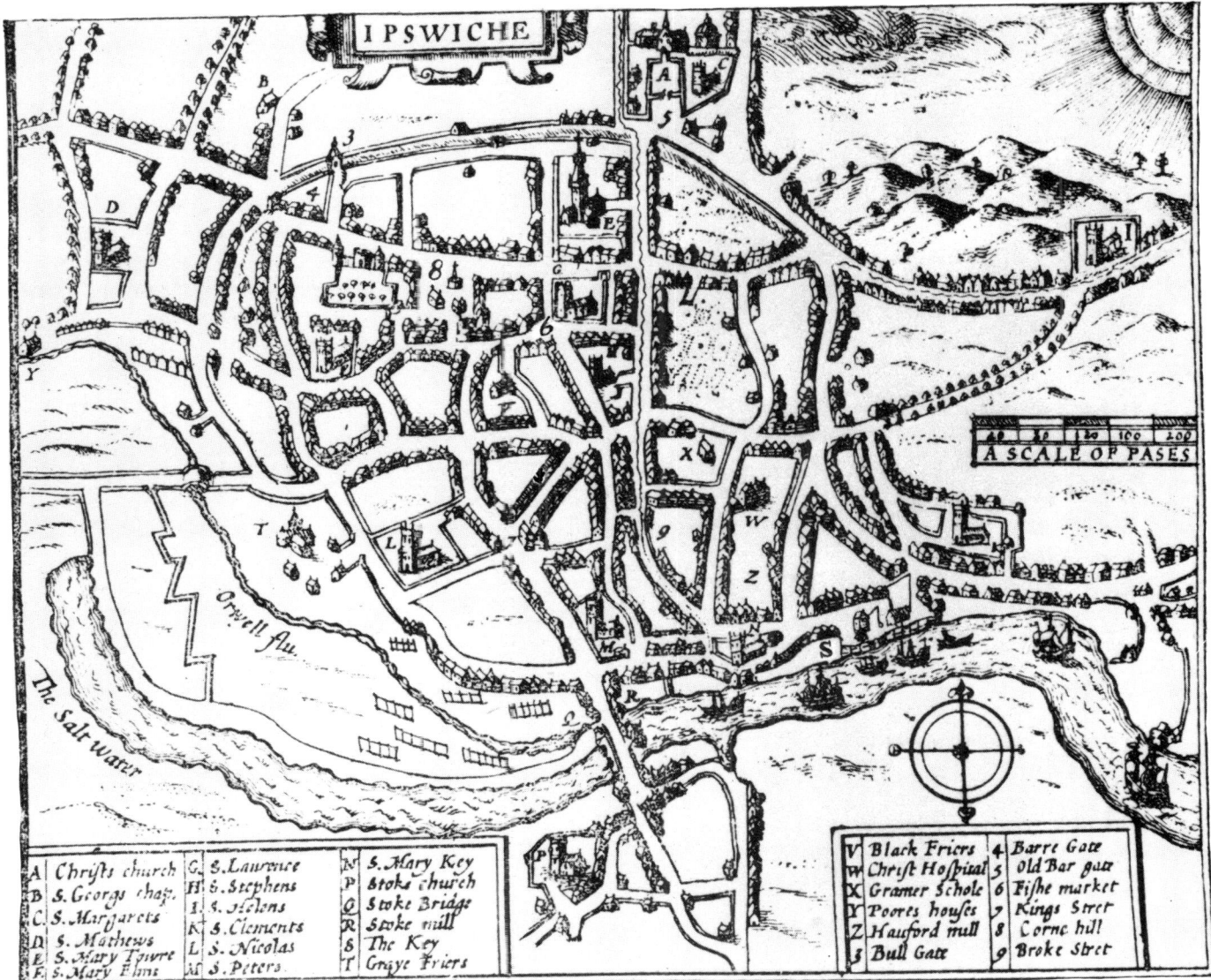

IPSWICHE

A	Chrifts church	G	S. Lawrence	N	S. Mary Key
B	S. Georgs chap.	H	S. Stephens	P	Stoke church
C	S. Margarets	I	S. Helens	Q	Stoke Bridge
D	S. Mathews	K	S. Clements	R	Stoke mill
E	S. Mary Tovvre	L	S. Nicolas	S	The Key
F	S. Mary Elms	M	S. Peters	T	Graye Friers

V	Black Friers	4	Barre Gate
W	Chrift Hofpital	5	Old Bar gate
X	Gramer Schole	6	Fifhe market
Y	Poores houses	7	Kings Stret
Z	Hauford mull	8	Corne hill
3	Bull Gate	9	Broke Stret

B   **A map of seventeenth-century Ipswich**

1 Study picture **A**.
   (a) Name the town.
   (b) How was it described?
   (c) Why did it grow?
   (d) What goods were brought there?

2 What might happen in towns after young men had been drinking, and how did travellers protect themselves?

3 Look at map **B** and answer these questions.
   (a) What would people buy at 6 and 8?
   (b) Where would the sick, poor and scholars go?
   (c) What is happening at The Key (S)?
   (d) What can you see to the north of St Helen's (I)?
   (e) What do you notice about the houses?

4 Draw a frieze of a street in a Stuart town (use all the information in the chapter to help you).

39 Transport

In Stuart times travel was usually difficult and often dangerous. Many people walked a great deal, even over large distances, because they could not afford to travel any other way. Some went on horseback and horses could be hired at inns.

Merchants transported their goods on pack-horses, which could carry about seventy kilos weight each. These horses travelled in gangs, sometimes fifty in number. All over Britain the 'packmen' carried such goods as wool and hops (fruit used for flavouring beer), butter and fish on their way to market.

Other goods were carried in stage-waggons, which also held passengers. The wheels were broad and the 'stagers' were pulled by six or eight horses. Yet progress was slow, sometimes only about twenty kilometres a day. For example, a journey from London to Liverpool could take ten days even in a good summer.

In London, hackney coaches could be hired for the day from inns and became popular with well-to-do people. The coachman sat on one of his horses, carrying a short whip, and drove his fare-paying passengers about the city.

Stage coaches were first used about 1640. Usually they were pulled by four horses and carried six or eight inside passengers, as well as some outside. The horses worked in teams which were replaced at 'stages', usually inns about thirty-five kilometres apart.

There were dangers from highwaymen. They knew the times of coaches and could learn from a friendly inn-keeper which traveller might be worth robbing. So they waited for their wealthy victims at isolated spots on the journey – and then held up the coach.

Roads were extremely bad. Each parish had to maintain its own section but often neglected the work. Thus the trackways were sometimes covered with mud in winter, or pitted with ruts in summer.

From 1663 Turnpike Acts were passed. These set up toll-gates where money was paid by those who used the road. This money was used for the upkeep and repair of the road.

As Britain has many rivers, travel by water was often safer and faster than by land. Goods and people were transported in boats and barges between some inland towns. Also, many small ships carried cargo and passengers around the coast.

At the end of Stuart times, travel in Britain was still slow. A journey could be a great ordeal.

A A travelling coach, used by rich people

B A stage waggon, used to carry goods and passengers

Things to do

1   List ten ways in which you can travel today.

2   Study all the pictures in this chapter and list the ways in which people travelled or carried goods in Stuart times.

3   (a) Who or what were 'packmen', 'stagers' and 'stages'?
    (b) Draw a picture of one of these.
    (c) List two dangers of travelling by road.

4   (a) Look at picture **D**. Explain why there is a gate across the road.
    (b) Why were these toll-gates set up?

5   (a) Was there a faster and safer way of travelling than by road?
    (b) How would you prefer to have travelled in Stuart times – by road or by water? Give reasons for your answer.

D A toll-gate where people using the road would have to pay for the privilege

C Bristol in the seventeenth century. Notice the use of sledges and pack-horses

40 Gregory King

In 1688 a writer named Gregory King made a study of all the people in England. Those were the days before computers and telephones, daily newspapers and government forms. Therefore some of his figures could not be proved completely correct. However, we know that he was nearly right.

He said that there were about 5,500,000 people altogether. One tenth of these lived in London, which was the largest capital in Europe. More than 4,000,000 men, women and children lived in the small villages and hamlets which were dotted across the countryside. For all of them life was simpler – and shorter – than today's. Much of it was lived round the farming year, with the planting, growing and harvesting of crops playing an important part in everyone's existence.

Gregory King placed people on a pyramid, according to their wealth and position in life at that time. At the very base were some 30,000 vagrants who had no wealth. He described them as thieves, beggars and gipsies, who were not welcome either in town or country.

He then listed over 2,500,000 people as labourers, cottagers or paupers. Many of these were farm workers, servants or miners. Some had rights to small pieces of land which they rented, and nearly half of them received extra money because they were poor. This extra was a kind of social security, paid from parish funds.

Above them he showed over 2,000,000 citizens and their families who were better off. They included military and naval officers and craftsmen; there were also farmers and people who owned their own land.

Going up the pyramid he then placed clergymen, and lawyers, merchants and

Sections of society	Income per year	'Total number of people 5,495,520'
Poor families	£12 – £15	2,825,000
Tenant farmers and their families	£40 – £100	1,730,000
Merchants, tradesmen and craftsmen	£22 – £600	564,000
Professional families (clergy, lawyers etc . . .)	£50 – £100	223,000
Nobility and gentry	£200 – £20,000	153,520

A   Gregory King's chart

government officials. Some of these were quite rich, because a merchant could earn about £200 a year while a servant might receive only £15 for the same period of work.

On the top of his list Gregory King placed lords and bishops, together with knights and squires. They held great power in the government. Many were very rich, especially from the land they owned. With their wealth they built fine houses and mansions, some of which still stand, and they enjoyed a high standard of living.

This was the England of 1688, only three centuries ago. What great changes there have been since then!

Things to do

1 Read the chapter and answer these
   questions:
   (a) When did Gregory King make a study of
       England?
   (b) How many people lived in England?
   (c) How many of these lived in London?
   (d) Where did most people live?
   (e) What did most people do for a living?

2 (a) Rearrange these groups into order of
       wealth.
       1 Vagrants
       2 Lawyers
       3 Military officers
       4 Rich landowners
       5 Labourers
   (b) How many people were there in each of
       these groups?
   (The text and picture **A** will help you with this
   question.)

3 Study pictures **B** and **C**.
   (a) Write a few sentences about the life of
       the woman.
   (b) Write a few sentences about the lives of
       the owners of Eaton Hall.

4 (a) What were almshouses (picture **D**)?
   (b) What other help did poor people get?

B A vagrant (homeless) family in London.
People such as these, with no income, drifted
in from the country looking for work

C Eaton Hall, Cheshire. A very few people at
the top of Gregory King's 'pyramid' lived in
such splendour

D Almshouses. Generous people would build
and maintain accommodation such as this for
the old and the sick

41 The British overseas

Some English people settled in the New World seeking better chances in life. Many emigrated for religious reasons. So during Stuart times English colonies grew in number along the eastern coast of North America.

In 1634 Maryland was founded as a Catholic colony. Roman Catholics who went there had freedom to practise their religion without fear of punishment.

Later, more settlements were made on the same coast. Carolina was established in 1663. In the next year the Dutch colony of New Amsterdam was captured and renamed New York. After the end of Charles II's reign Pennsylvania was founded. Altogether, twelve of the original thirteen colonies began during Stuart times.

These settlements soon became important for their trade. Tobacco and cotton were grown and brought good profits. There was timber for houses and ships. The colonists bought many manufactured goods from Britain.

It was generally believed that colonies existed for the good of the mother-country, and strict control was kept over their trade. Navigation Acts were passed in England which laid down that goods intended for trading with the colonies were to be carried only in English ships. Also, some goods from the colonies could be exported only to England.

West Indian islands also were taken for settlement. The most important was Barbados (1625) where sugar was grown. In Cromwell's time Jamaica was captured (1655) from the Spaniards.

Cotton, sugar and tobacco plantations needed labour, so slaves were taken from Africa and sold in the New World. Some English captains

A The sugar plantations of the West Indies enabled European merchants to become very rich

made great profits from buying and selling black people, who were transported across the Atlantic Ocean. English companies were formed to control the trade from West Africa.

Another area of English settlement was the Spice Islands of the Far East. However, the East India Company, set up in 1600, quarrelled with the Dutch, who were great trading rivals. In 1623 English merchants were driven out by the Dutch.

But in India itself some successful settlements were made. Trading posts were started on various parts of the coast, where merchants bought and sold goods. In Charles II's reign the East India Company gained the important trading centre of Bombay.

Thus by the end of Stuart times England had an empire overseas. A growing number of Englishmen went to these lands either as traders, or to live permanently.

Things to do

1 Study picture **B**
   (a) Who is person *1*?
   (b) Which American colony was named after him?
   (c) What was his religion?
   (d) Name the Indian tribe.
   (e) Name three other American colonies.

2 Study map **C** then copy and complete the following lists:

   British colonies and trading posts
   New England

   Spanish colonies and trading posts
   New Spain (Mexico)

3 (a) What product came from the West Indies?
   (b) Name two important West Indian islands.
   (c) Why were slaves taken from Africa?

B William Penn signing a peace treaty with the Delaware Indians. Pennsylvania was established in 1681 for the Quakers (a religious group)

4 Write a few sentences on the English settlement of India.

5 Make a list of arguments (a) for and (b) against a country having colonies.

C Major European colonial settlements in the seventeenth century

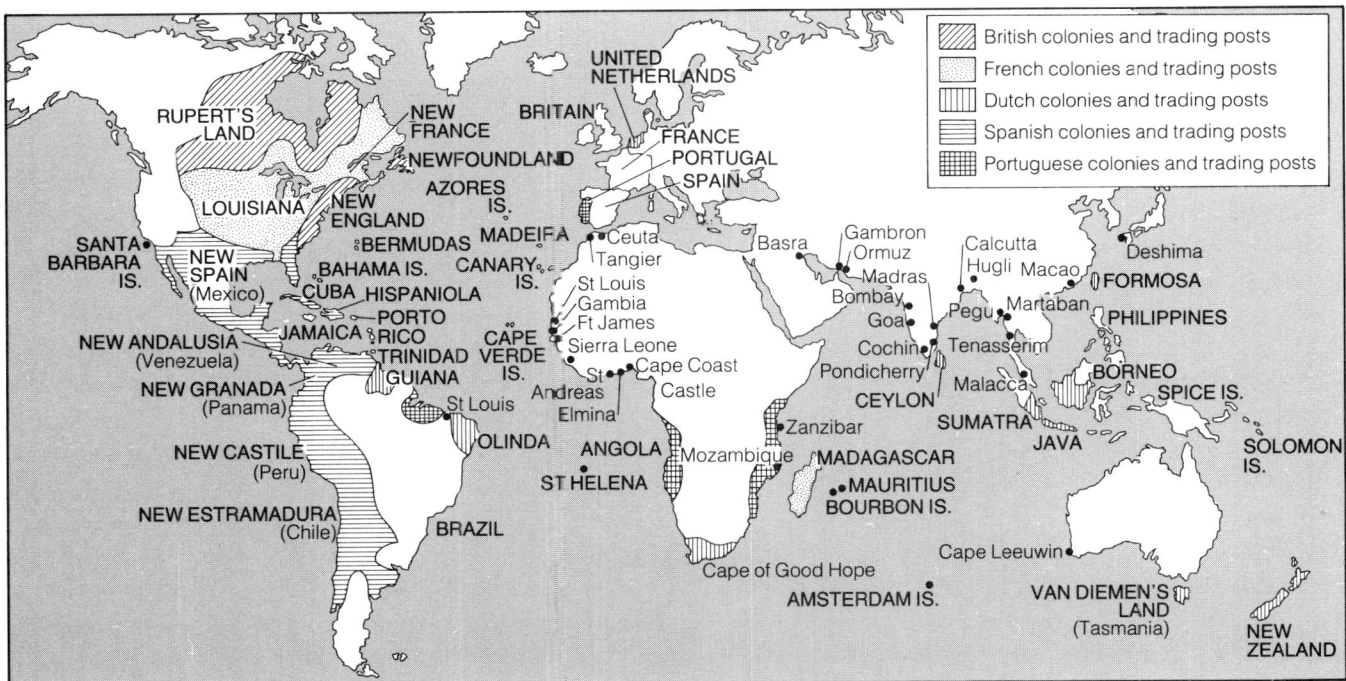

42 James II and the Glorious Revolution

James II was very different from his brother, Charles II, whom he succeeded in 1685. Charles often disagreed with Parliament but was careful and tactful enough to avoid a desperate quarrel. James, on the other hand, had such an argument that he was driven from the throne after only three years.

Soon after he became king there was a Protestant rebellion led by the Duke of Monmouth, who was the illegitimate son of Charles II. This uprising was crushed and those rebels still alive were either hanged or transported abroad.

The king was worried and kept a strong army to guard against future rebellions. 20,000 soldiers assembled every year at Hounslow Heath, and the number of Catholic officers in the army increased.

Many English people did not like the way in which James tried to give more rights to Catholics. There was a chance that religious trouble would break out again and the tragedies of the Civil War were still in people's memories.

Matters came to a head in 1688. James's first wife, Anne Hyde, had died in 1671, leaving two daughters, Mary and Anne. Both were Protestant and thus Catholic rule would end when the king died.

But James had married again: an Italian Catholic, Mary of Modena. In June 1688, she gave birth to a son. He was the new heir to the throne, and Protestants felt that their cause was lost.

James's daughter, Mary, was married to a Dutch Protestant prince, William of Orange. Parliament now invited him to come to England and take the throne. William therefore raised an army, sailed for England and landed in Devon. Realizing that his people were not loyal

A James II, a brave soldier but a king whose actions disturbed Parliament and Protestants

to him, James took a ship to France in December 1688, and never returned.

Mary and William ruled jointly. As the overthrow of James was made with little trouble, the event is sometimes called 'The Glorious Revolution', or 'The Bloodless Revolution'.

Since Parliament wanted to cut the monarch's strength, William and Mary had to sign the Bill of Rights, which limited their power. For example, monarchs could not impose taxes without Parliament's agreement. Laws made by Parliament could not be altered by monarchs, who were also not allowed to keep a standing army.

Thus the power of English kings was cut and the strength of Parliament grew.

Things to do

1 Read the chapter and answer these questions:
   (a) Who became king after Charles II?
   (b) What relation was he to Charles II?
   (c) When did the new king succeed Charles II?
   (d) Who rebelled against the new king?
   (e) What happened to the rebels?

2 Study picture **B** and paragraphs *8* and *9*.
   (a) What is happening in the picture?
   (b) What was the overthrow of James II called?
   (c) What document did William and Mary sign?
   (d) What could a monarch not do?
   (e) Who gained most from the revolution?

3 Copy picture **C** into your book.

Charles I = Henrietta Maria of France

Charles II   Mary of Modena = James II = Anne Hyde

James (born 1688)   Mary = William of Orange   Anne

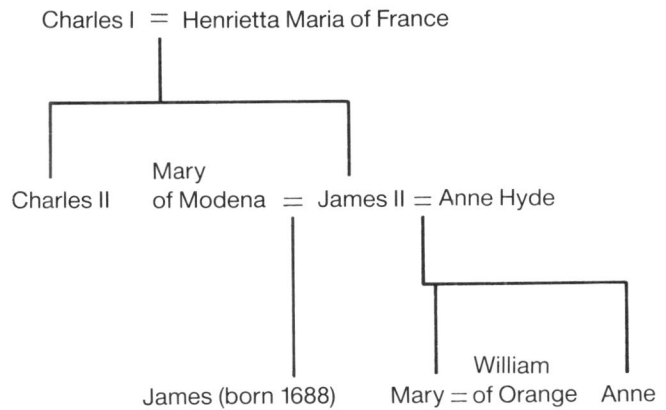

C | **The family tree of James II**

4 Explain in your own words why the birth of a son to Mary of Modena in 1688 would please English Catholics but distress Protestants.

B | **A representative of Parliament offers the crown of England to both William and Mary. The Divine Right of kings was at an end**

43 John Churchill, Duke of Marlborough

In England's history there have been many famous sailors, explorers and admirals, but few well-known generals. One of the most successful was John Churchill, who was born in 1650.

During the Civil War his father supported the king, losing wealth and position for doing so. After leaving school John became an officer in the Foot Guards and soon learned about the methods of war. From 1688 to 1690 he saw service in Tangier, Morocco, and later fought against the Dutch.

Back in England he fell in love with Sarah Jennings, a lady-in-waiting to the Duchess of York. Sarah was hot-tempered and tried to dominate others, while Churchill was easy-going and good-natured. They were perfectly happy together.

When William of Orange drove James II from the throne in 1688, Churchill supported William. He was rewarded with a title – the Earl of Marlborough (he became a Duke later), yet he continued to write to James II, who was living abroad. There was a chance that the Stuarts might return so Churchill wanted to guard his own interests. Some people did not like this side of his character.

When Anne became queen in 1702 both Marlborough and his wife were her firm friends and held high positions. He was a leading soldier, while Sarah influenced the queen at Court.

Marlborough was Captain-General of the forces. At that time England's greatest enemies were the French, who threatened to dominate Europe. Thus Marlborough was soon involved in fighting them and proved to be a successful commander.

A The Churchills and their family. Marlborough was courageous, patient and charming. His wife Sarah had a strong personality

Over the next few years he won four great victories against the French, though sometimes at heavy cost. They were at Blenheim (1704), Ramillies (1706), Oudenarde (1708) and Malplaquet (1709). The Duke's name became known all over Europe.

Parliament voted a large sum of money to build a house for him. This was the magnificent Blenheim Palace, erected at Woodstock in Oxfordshire, which still stands. It was a present from the nation.

But the war dragged on, and later Marlborough and his wife fell out of favour with the queen. In 1713 peace was made when the Treaty of Utrecht was signed with the French and the Duke's career was at an end. He died nine years later and was buried in St Paul's Cathedral.

At his death Sarah wrote in her Bible: 'Today died the best man that ever lived.'

Things to do

1 Read the chapter carefully and explain what happened on each of the following dates:
   (a) 1650
   (b) 1688–90
   (c) 1688
   (d) 1704
   (e) 1722

2 Answer **true** or **false**:
   (a) Churchill's father was a Royalist in the Civil War.
   (b) Sarah Jennings was easy-going and good-natured.
   (c) Churchill supported William of Orange.
   (d) Queen Anne disliked the Marlboroughs.
   (e) Marlborough won famous victories over the French.

3 Study picture **B**.
   (a) Who were Marlborough's allies at the battle?
   (b) Who were his opponents?
   (c) Why was the battle so important?

B Marlborough at Blenheim. Supported by Prince Eugene of Austria, Marlborough defeated Marshall Tallard of France. A French victory would have enabled Louis XIV of France to invade Holland

4 Re-read the chapter and study all the captions to the pictures. Write out two lists – (a) Marlborough's good points and (b) Marlborough's bad points.

C Blenheim Palace was given to the Marlboroughs by Queen Anne. Sarah quarrelled fiercely with Vanbrugh, the architect

44 Queen Anne

Anne succeeded to the throne in March 1702 and was crowned in the next month. She was thirty-seven years old and had been married for some years to Prince George of Denmark. The queen was not an attractive woman. She was large, fat and suffered from ill-health. During her life she gave birth to sixteen children, all of whom died. Her last surviving son, the young Duke of Gloucester, had died in 1700, so the Act of Settlement had to be passed to arrange the succession when she died.

At the start of her reign the queen was very friendly with the Duchess of Marlborough. Anne was not a brilliant woman, being slow in many ways, and the Duchess often dominated her with her own point of view. They made up names for talking and writing to each other. Anne called the Duchess 'Mrs Freeman' and was herself known as 'Mrs Morley'.

In 1707 an important event occurred in British history. After 1688 some people wanted one single Parliament for both England and Scotland. From 1603 each country had its own Parliament, although the two countries had been part of one kingdom. There was opposition to the proposed union in both countries, but all the objections were put aside. The Scots were given forty-five seats in the House of Commons and sixteen in the House of Lords. Since then the single Parliament has governed both countries.

Queen Anne grew ill in 1714. Her health had been poor all through the reign; now it became worse and it was soon obvious that she was dying. At this stage there was a great deal of argument between the two political parties – Whigs and Tories. Much of it was connected with who should rule next. The Act of Settlement had agreed that a Protestant German from Hanover, who had a claim to the throne, should take over.

However, some people did not like the idea of offering the British crown to a German. They wanted it to go to James II's son, who lived abroad, yet claimed that he was the rightful king.

Anne died in July 1714 while the argument was going on. All her children were already dead, so the royal House of Stuart came to an end. A new era, the Georgian age, was about to begin.

A A London coffee house in the early eighteenth century. Notice the newspapers. Here men would discuss politics and often get into arguments

Things to do

B Queen Anne surrounded by her ministers

1 Study picture **B** after having read the chapter.
   (a) Who is person *1*?
   (b) How old was she in 1702?
   (c) Describe person *1*.
   (d) To whom was she married?
   (e) Why was an Act of Settlement passed?

2 Who was: (a) Mrs Morley; and (b) Mrs Freeman?

3 Study picture **C**.
   (a) Who is the boy?
   (b) Whose son was he?
   (c) Did he have a claim to the throne?
   (d) Why could he not be king?
   (e) Where did he live in 1714?

4 Imagine you are in the London coffee house in picture **A**. Explain to your friend why you think it is a good idea to have one Parliament for England and Scotland.

5 (a) Who was to succeed Anne when she died?
   (b) Why did some people object to this?

C The children of James II – Prince James and Princess Louise. As a Catholic, the prince was not allowed to succeed his father as king

45 Looking back

Tudor and Stuart times were really a short period in British history. They lasted for two and a quarter centuries. Yet in that time some most important events occurred in the nation's story and they affect people still today. Here, then, is a reminder of some of them.

Remember that the Tudor family took the throne in 1485 after winning a battle which ended a war. Peace was restored to England. Then came the great religious troubles of the sixteenth century, bringing arguments between Catholics and Protestants. These developed in the reign of Henry VIII and continued while his son, Edward VI, and his daughter, Mary I, were on the throne.

The age of Elizabeth was one of the greatest in English history, a time of famous writers and seamen. Few monarchs have been loved so much by their people as 'Good Queen Bess'. Danger came from a rival queen, Mary, Queen of Scots. It also came from abroad as there were clashes between explorers sailing on journeys from Europe to other parts of the world.

With the arrival of James I on the English throne, argument developed between kings and their Parliaments. Who should control the government of the country? This led to a Civil War in the middle of the seventeenth century. The struggle was long and bitter and ended with the execution of the king.

For eleven years Parliament ruled and the Puritans governed England. Then the son of the beheaded king was offered the crown – and England has remained a monarchy ever since.

Other events were imprinted on the nation's story. The Plague was a disaster which showed the low standards of health and cleanliness at that time. The Fire was a great tragedy, yet produced some good when parts of London were rebuilt with the splendid architecture of Christopher Wren.

Then came more troubles with the sovereign when the Catholic James II was forced off the throne and replaced by Protestant William and Mary. And as the Stuarts came to an end with the death of Queen Anne, another problem loomed up. Who should succeed next?

Wherever you live in Britain the legacy of the Tudors and Stuarts can be seen. There are houses and churches, memorials and castles, books and furniture. Make sure that in your lifetime you guard the legacy carefully, then hand it on to your descendants.

MONARCH AND HOUSE	REIGNED
The House of York	
Edward IV	1461-1483
Edward V	1483
Richard III	1483-1485
The House of Tudor	
Henry VII	1485-1509
Henry VIII	1509-1547
Edward VI	1547-1553
Mary I	1553-1558
Elizabeth I	1558-1603
The House of Stuart	
James I (VI of Scotland)	1603-1625
Charles I	1625-1649 (beheaded)
Commonwealth declared	*May, 1649*
Oliver Cromwell, Lord Protector,	*1653-1658*
Richard Cromwell, Lord Protector,	*1658-1659*
Charles II (restored 1660)	1649-1685
James II (VII of Scotland)	1685-1688 (deposed)
William III and Mary II	1689-1702 (Mary died 1694)
Anne	1702-1714

A Kings and Queens 1461–1714

Things to do

1 Look at picture **A**.
   (a) How many royal families were there between 1461 and 1714?
   (b) Which family reigned for the longest time?
   (c) Which monarch reigned for the longest time?

2 Write down one sentence for each of the following monarchs to say why each will be remembered. (Refer back to the relevant chapters.)
   (a) Henry VII
   (b) Henry VIII
   (c) Elizabeth I
   (d) Charles I
   (e) James II

3 Which of the following events was, in your opinion, the most important? Give reasons for your answer. (You may need to look back to the relevant chapters.)
   (a) Henry VII becoming King of England
   (b) The Renaissance
   (c) The Reformation
   (d) The defeat of the Armada
   (e) The colonization of America

4 Write a few sentences on each of the three most interesting people you have read about in this book.

5 Are there any houses, churches, palaces or battlefields in your area which date from the Tudor or Stuart period? Write a brief, illustrated description of one which interests you.

B Episodes in Tudor and Stuart history

Henry Tudor being crowned after the Battle of Bosworth, 1485

The Defeat of the Spanish Armada, 1588

The Gunpowder Plot, 1605

The execution of Charles I, 1649

Charles II returns triumphantly to London, 1660

The Fire of London, 1666

Acknowledgements

Aerofilms Ltd: 89(C); A F Kersting 72(A); Amsterdams Historisch Museum: 71(C); Ashmolean Museum: 54(B); B A Seaby Ltd: 53(B); BBC Hulton Picture Library: 5(C), 14(A), 23(C), 26(A), 27(B), 28(A), 29(B), 34(A), 35(C), 37(D), 40(B), 41(C), 53(C), 55(E), 61(C), 63(C), 75(C), 81(D), 84(A), 87(B), 91(B); Bildarchiv Foto Marburg: 13(B); Bradford Art Galleries and Museums: 42(B); British Library: 5(D), 70(A) British Museum: 8(A), 25(B), 34(B), 36(B), 43(C), 51(C), 53(D), 55(E), 60(A), 63(D), 65(C), 77(C); B T Batsford: 25(C), 45(B), 78(A), 83(C), 83(D), 90(A); Burrel Collection: 25(D); City of Bristol Museum and Art Gallery: 81(C); The Dean and Chapter of Canterbury Cathedral: 6(B); English Heritage: 16(A); Evans Bros Ltd: 21(B); Fortean Picture Library: 77(B); Fotomas Index: 4(B), 23(B); 24(A); The Frick Collection: 38(A); By permission of the Duke of Grafton and the Cortauld Institute of Art: 62(B); Hamlyn Publishing Group: 39(C); Hector Innes: 27(C); By permission of the Head Master and Governors of King Edward VI School, Stratford-upon-Avon. Photograph by Jarrold and Sons Ltd: 40(A); Kunsthistorisches Museum: 15(C); The Master and Fellows of Magdalene College Cambridge: 67(B); Mansell Collection: 9(D), 11(B), 11(C), 17(B), 18(A), 30(B), 31(E), 33(C), 44(A), 47(B), 47(C), 49(B), 49(C), 51(D), 54(A), 55(C), 58(A), 59(C), 68(A), 69(B), 74(A), 75(D), 80(A), 80(B), 83(B); Mary Evans Picture Library: 59(B), 62(A), 75(B); Museo del Prado, Madrid: 22(A); Museum of English Rural Life: 76(A); National Galleries of Scotland: 27(D); National Gallery of Ireland: 37(C); National Maritime Museum: 31(C), 31(D), 71(B); National Monuments Record and B T Batsford Ltd: 38(B); National Portrait Gallery: 7(C), 8(B), 14(B), 15(D), 17(C), 20(A), 23(D), 46(A), 51(B), 52(A), 55(D), 61(B), 64(A), 86(A), 91(C); National Trust: 42(A); Oeffentliche Kunstsammlung Base: 17(D); Portsmouth and Sunderland Newspapers Plc: 19(C); Royal Library: 10(A); Society of Antiquaries: 69(C); Suffolk County Council 79(B); Swan AV Library: 85(B); Thomas Photos, Oxford: 73(B); Victoria and Albert Museum: 45(C); Wayland Picture Library: 48(A); Weaver-Smith Collection: 67(C); Weidenfield (Publishers) Ltd: 33(B); Wellcome Institute Library: 66(A); Jeremy Whitaker and Duke of Marlborough: 88(A), 89(B).

Illustrations by Ray Burrows
Maps by Rodney Paull
Picture Research by Audrey Daly

Although every effort has been made to trace and obtain correct copyright information, the Publishers would be pleased to hear from copyright holders regarding any omissions or inaccuracies.

Index